Heritage
APPLES

Heritage APPLES

Caroline Ball

Bodleian Library
UNIVERSITY OF OXFORD

First published in 2019 by the Bodleian Library
Broad Street, Oxford OX1 3BG
www.bodleianshop.co.uk

ISBN 978 1 85124 516 1

The Publisher is very grateful to Bernwode Nurseries for their kind permission
to use material from www.bernwodeplants.co.uk in this book.

Cover design by Dot Little at the Bodleian Library
Designed and typeset in 11½ on 16 Monotype Baskerville by illuminati, Grosmont
Printed and bound by C&C Offset Printing Co. Ltd on 140 gsm Chinese GS woodfree paper

British Library Catalogue in Publishing Data
A CIP record of this publication is available from the British Library

Contents

Introduction

'Good apple pies are a considerable part of our domestic happiness', wrote Jane Austen to her sister Cassandra in 1815. And we might say 'good apples' too, for they have been a staple of the domestic scene since – well, since considerably before Miss Austen put pen to paper. Indeed, the oldest variety of apple held by the National Fruit Collection in Brogdale, Kent, is said to have been brought over to England by a Roman general.

Whether this particular apple, the Decio, can really be traced quite so far back may be open to question, but the Romans certainly introduced apple trees to this northern outpost of empire, and their larger, sweeter fruit were a huge improvement on the tiny native crab apples that had formed part of the Britons' diet since Neolithic times. The British took to apples, and apples took to Britain, which provided an ideal combination of climate and terrain.

Although apples are not native to Britain, they have been part of our lives for so long that they have bedded down not only into our cuisine but into our language. An apple a day keeps the doctor away. A darling is the apple of your eye. If you put a spanner in the works, you upset the apple cart. A rosy, round-faced child has apple cheeks. A wrong sort is a bad apple, rotten to the core.

Another saying is that you can't compare apples and pears. But apples themselves are not even similar to each other; in fact, some superficially look more like pears! Centuries of accidental and deliberate hybridization

Cider apples from *The Herefordshire Pomona*.

have resulted in an enormous diversity. The National Fruit Collection has a 'living library' of some 2,000 varieties, and many more in its database. These range from dainty 'lady' apples, considered neat enough to sit in a lady's purse or pocket, to boastful big boys such as Lewis's Incomparable and Catshead, and from honey-sweet dessert apples to mouth-puckering cider apples, and apples that taste of pineapple, or banana, or aniseed…

However, unless you are already an apple addict, you will have come across few of these and tasted even fewer. English Apples and Pears, a company that represents the bulk of English commercial growers, reports that its members grow just a couple of dozen different varieties, and only about a third of these are what might be termed traditional English. What a different picture Hannah Glasse conjured up 250 years ago in *The Art of Cookery Made Plain and Easy*. As an aid to menu-planning she provided month-by-month lists of what should be available in the kitchen garden or stores. Her list of apples for January alone reads:

> the Kentish, russet, golden, French, kirton and Dutch pippins, John apples, winter queenings, the marigold and Harvey apples, pom-water, golden-dorset, renneting, love's pearmain, and the winter-pearmain.

How did it come to pass that less than 2 per cent of surviving British apples are now grown in commercial quantities, and does this mean that before long 'apple' will connote a single type rather than a rich medley of shapes and flavours? Or has the tide turned? First, a little history.

From the Mountains of Heaven

The British may like to think of the apple as quintessentially theirs, although the Germans and Austrians, among others, also claim it as their national fruit, but its origins are far, far to the east. Much research has gone into where the earliest apple trees came from and their journey

'An Early ripe Apple and good in taste', from 'The Tradescants' Orchard'. Oxford, Bodleian Library, MS. Ashmole 1461, fol. 127r.

An Early ripe Apple
and good in taste.

August 22

to our orchards. Two thousand years ago apples came into the Roman Empire from its eastern border and for a long time it was believed that the birthplace of the apple was the region to the south and east of present-day Turkey, the Caucasus mountains and the Fertile Crescent, where many of our staple grains and plants originated. Identifiable remains of apples discovered in Jordan and Asian Turkey have been found to be over 8,000 years old. However, twentieth-century researches pushed the apple's sources still further east, and more recent DNA testing has confirmed that *Malus sieversii*, the common ancestor of today's domesticated apples, originated in the fruit forests of the Kyrgyzstan–Kazakhstan–China border, in particular the Tien Shan, the 'Mountains of Heaven'. These once extensive fruit forests have shrunk to a few scattered pockets, but at the heart of this area is the Almaty region of Kazakhstan, whose former capital, Alma Ata, tellingly translates as 'Father of Apples'.

Growers learnt early on that apples did not come true from seed – apples with 'Pippin' in their name indicate that they arose by happy chance from sowing an apple pip – and few rooted successfully from cuttings, so grafting became the chosen method of propagation. As it still is (*see page 222*). Over the past two millennia, domestic apples have diversified in shape, size, taste and habit, by either natural or deliberate cross-breeding. They have been bred to enhance qualities such as size, flavour, storing qualities and resistance to disease, especially that curse of apples, the codling moth ('codling' or 'codlin' was once a widely used term for apples, especially those that cooked to a soft fluff).

The apple not only hybridizes easily but is highly adaptable. Just as the Romans had established it throughout much of their empire, the British colonialists did the same, and North America, Australasia, South Africa, even the cooler regions of India came to grow apples in abundance. Although sometimes saplings were taken abroad and propagated, the most

Plan for a garden from William Lawson, *A New Orchard and Garden*, 1623.

convenient method of shipping and disseminating fruit trees was as pips, so the trees that grew from them were distinct from their parents. Every country developed its own distinct apple heritage.

Our Georgian and Victorian forebears had the most marvellous array of apples to choose from, and appreciated different varieties through the seasons. Seldom, however, did they get to taste apples from far beyond their own locale. The great estates of course traded their knowledge and their fruit, but in the preindustrial era transporting fruit that spoilt easily was a problem, so in orchards and gardens from Kent to Kilkenny, Cornwall to Clydesdale, there flourished varieties that had been developed to suit their own local conditions but were largely unknown elsewhere.

But this was changing. The Industrial Revolution, the migration from the countryside to towns, the breaking up of many great estates in the wake of the First World War, the arrival of refrigeration – all contributed to changing demands on the humble apple. Apples that lasted only a week or two once picked lost out to those that could be stored through the winter; tougher-skinned varieties were preferred over easy bruisers; trees that were overlarge, gangly or prone to disease lost ground to neater, easier to manage, higher-yielding relations. In the course of this adaptation to the modern world much was gained but a crucial thing was lost: variety.

As transport continued to improve and agriculture became mechanized, certain varieties showed their superiority and became the apples of choice among commercial growers. What was the point of investing in an apple that was too small and fiddly to pick in quantity, even if it made the most delicious cider? Why lose money growing an apple, however wonderfully flavoured, if it wouldn't survive the journey to market? In the course of the twentieth century this trend intensified. Small orchards became commercially unviable and larger growers believed it made sound sense to concentrate on fewer varieties that ticked as many boxes as possible. In addition, back gardens shrank, it became easier to buy fruit and veg in one-stop supermarkets than to grow your own, and the food market became

Gardeners toiling in an orchard. Woodcut illustration from William Lawson,
A New Orchard and Garden, 1623. Oxford, Bodleian Library, Lawn e. 8.

a global one. The biggest-selling apples today – Braeburn, Jazz, Pink Lady
and Gala – are known as the Antipodean Four as they were all bred in
Australia and New Zealand.

Increasing homogeneity has repercussions on two particular aspects of
appledom: genetics and flavour.

Although new varieties are still regularly appearing on the market, they
are often bred from the same small gene pool (Jazz is a Gala x Braeburn
cross, for example). Does this matter? The banana is a warning that it does.
Bananas (like apples) are propagated vegetatively rather than by seed. This
has effectively led to all bananas bred commercially for consumption in the
West being not only the same variety, the Cavendish, but clones of each
other. Were a disease to attack the banana, then the entire world's crop
would be vulnerable, as there would be no commercially grown alternative
that might be resistant. Panama disease now poses just such a threat. This

7

sword of Damocles hanging over the future of the banana is a warning, especially when breeding fruit that is vegetatively propagated. It is not just among humans that inbreeding is a bad idea.

Flavour is a more subjective area. Were they more flavoursome, the apples of our childhood, of the Victorians, of Shakespeare? Not necessarily. A great many old varieties fell by the wayside because they were woolly or sour or just tasteless. But what we have lost, or forgotten, is the variance in taste from one apple to another – the vast difference between the rich fruitiness of Court of Wick, the unexpected anise of Cellini or the strawberry sweetness of a fresh Devonshire Quarrenden. And, as we know and expect of wine but usually overlook in apples, flavour changes with maturity. Even that favourite, Cox's Orange Pippin, is often picked too early and experienced as a bland, immature version of its ideal self.

From such gloom, however, the prognosis is brightening. The twenty-first century has witnessed a revival of interest in the food we eat: how it is grown, where it comes from and how it is treated. Local and seasonal are taking priority over convenient and uniform. Heritage apples are part of this movement.

Our heritage
There is a growing recognition that we should cherish our heritage apples – use them or lose them. Since 2007 orchards have been given priority status in the UK Biodiversity Action Plan, and pomologists have encouraged the rediscovery and propagation of many old varieties that were either in peril of disappearing or believed already lost to cultivation. Years can be spent on a frustrating roller coaster of a ride tracking down and identifying 'lost' apples, and DNA fingerprinting has added and removed a number of question marks over apple identification in recent years. Verification and reclassification go on.

While this book focuses on historic apples, dedicated breeders continue to seek out and develop interesting and characterful new varieties. Some

8

apples are bred for a specific purpose, such as Winter Gem, a variety with good disease resistance developed in the 1990s by the modern English apple breeder Hugh Ermen with the organic gardener in mind. Others are an accident of nature. A few years ago, a variety which came to be known as Christmas Pippin was discovered growing by the roadside; it was found to have so many virtues that it has been bred commercially. Tomorrow's heritage?

At the back of this book you'll find a few ideas of how to find and taste heritage apples for yourself. Community orchards are springing up; individual enthusiasts are planting 'hobby' orchards; restaurants are seeking out unusual and local varieties to enhance their menus. The resurgence of farmers' markets is providing a new arena for sellers and buyers alike, while local fruit networks support the revival of regional varieties, reintroducing us to forgotten taste sensations and urging a much needed diversity. In 1990 the organization Common Ground initiated Apple Day, now celebrated each year around 21 October, with tasting events and orchard open days increasing in popularity all over the country.

This book aims to encourage this renaissance. It is not a directory containing every available apple (others have done that admirable job), but instead takes as its inspiration a classic masterpiece of the fruit world: *The Herefordshire Pomona*.

The Herefordshire Pomona and the apples in this book

The beautiful and now rare and highly prized *Herefordshire Pomona* had surprisingly modest beginnings. It arose from a discussion in 1872 among members of the Woolhope Naturalists' Field Club (which still meets today) out on a fungus foray, on which they observed the deterioration of many of the local orchards. As the original introduction to the *Pomona* noted: 'celebrated as Herefordshire is for its orchards it was very remarkable that so few of the best varieties of apples should appear in the markets, or in the shops of Hereford.' *Plus ça change…*

9

This observation quickened the interest of the Club's members in growing choice varieties of apples, leading to apple shows and, in turn, the ambition to produce a new *Pomona*. A precedent had already been set: in 1811, the leading fruit breeder Thomas Andrew Knight had compiled the *Pomona Herefordiensis*, with engravings by William Hooker (the botanical artist, not the first director of Kew Gardens, with whom he is often confused). Such finely illustrated fruit books, called after Pomona, the Roman goddess of gardens and orchards, were popular in the first half of the nineteenth century – Hooker had produced his own *Pomona Londoniensis* in 1818 – but they were expensive enterprises, colour printing being in its infancy.

The Woolhope Club did not have inexhaustible funds, but it had a supportive membership whose subscriptions helped underwrite the enterprise, and one of its founder members, the remarkably able Dr Henry Graves Bull, took on the general editorship. Other committee members included Dr Robert Hogg, fruit expert and secretary of the London (later to become Royal) Horticultural Society and the Rev. C.H. Bulmer, of the well-known local cider-making family.

The enthusiasm among the Woolhope members for promoting local apples coincided with a nationwide resurgence of interest in British apples. Apples had long been imported from France, but the second half of the nineteenth century also saw a huge increase in new varieties from the United States and Canada. Fruit growers the other side of the Atlantic had not been hampered by lack of land or historic practices and preferences; they sought to produce attractive, commercially viable varieties that could be propagated in quantity and provide not only for the home tables but for export too. The British were seduced by the handsome new fruits appearing on the market: crisp Northern Spy; huge, bright-red Wolf River; glowing Esopus Spitzenburg; scarlet Opalescent and Baldwin; and – supposedly George Washington's favourite – the Newtown Pippin.

In the face of this threat to the domestic apple market there arose, as has happened before and since, a reaction in the form of a 'Buy British' campaign. In support of this, in October 1883 the Royal Horticultural Society hosted a National Apple Congress, its declared purpose to examine 'the numerous varieties cultivated throughout the country, to correct their nomenclature, and to compare their merits'. Its hope was that, in garnering information and opinions from growers around the country, a consensus would emerge as to which varieties could best be grown and promoted to reclaim the ground lost to the North Americans. The response far exceeded the organizers' expectations. Despite stressing that 'there would be no competition and no prizes' and that the Congress was for information and educational purposes only, they received more than 10,000 consignments covering 1,545 varieties. And the public flocked to see 'the most important of our national fruits' – the British had fallen in love with their apples all over again.

This was the background against which *The Herefordshire Pomona* was compiled. While it is not completely devoid of North American varieties, the emphasis on British-bred (or historically long-resident European) varieties is evident, while imported apples that had recently become so popular are notable by their absence: no Northern Spy, no Newtown Pippin.

The first volume, published in 1876, consisted of just six plates and accompanying text, but by degrees it grew in size and ambition, until the seventh and final volume appeared in 1885. It had been decided to include varieties of apples and pears from all over the country, not just Herefordshire, and the completed *Pomona* comprised 77 plates depicting 432 fruits, 270 of them varieties of apple.

The sheer beauty of the *Pomona* is attributable to two factors: technological advances in printing and Dr Bull's special asset, his eldest daughter. Edith Bull was a talented watercolourist, and all but two of the apple 'portraits' in the *Pomona* were faithfully and beautifully rendered by Miss Bull and a fellow artist, Alice Ellis, a gold medallist graduate of the Bloomsbury School of Art. (It is notable that several great pomonas were illustrated by the daughters of their compilers.) Many of the paintings were of exhibits at the Woolhope Club's shows, so they were portrayed stalk down, following show-bench convention – should you find yourself wanting to reach out to the lifelike images and turn them right side up!

All the subtlety and detail of the original watercolours were reproduced with astonishing accuracy by a printing process, chromolithography, that was only slowly taking over from hand-coloured etchings as a means of presenting colour illustrations. Only 600 sets of the *Pomona* were published, and the surviving few today command many thousands of pounds.

The true worth of *The Herefordshire Pomona*, however, is what lies within. As well as presenting a collection of extraordinarily beautiful images, the *Pomona* gives us a snapshot in time of – as its full title boasts – 'the most esteemed kinds of apples and pears' of the latter half of the nineteenth century. Not all of these 'esteemed varieties' are still available, and some that are have historical rather than edible attractions. But increasing interest in our apple heritage makes us eager to learn about and grow varieties that have stood the test of time. Where better to start than with these outstanding volumes?

The apples featured here are a medley of the *Pomona*'s apples still worth growing today, with a few historical curiosities. They come in all shapes and sizes and have very different qualities – some can only be appreciated when eaten straight off the tree, whereas others will store well, changing character as they mature; some are ready for picking in July, while for others you will have to wait until October or November. The greatest range, however, is in their flavours, and flavour is something that can really only be experienced, not described. So I hope most of all that this celebration of the apple will encourage you to seek out local suppliers and orchards and to treat yourself to as many new apple sensations as possible.

A page from Gerard's *Herball*, 1597, one of the most famous botanical works in English, describing two different varieties of apple. Oxford, Bodleian Library, L 1.5 Med.

is so infinite, that we haue thought it not amisse, to vse the same order or method with Apples that we haue done with Peares, that is, to giue them seuerall titles in Latine and English, and one generall description for the whole.

1 *Malus Carbonaria.*
The Pome Water tree.

2 *Malus Carbonaria longo fructu.*
The Bakers ditch Apple tree.

❧ *The generall description.*

THe Apple tree hath a bodie or trunke commonly of a meane bignesse, not very high, hauing long armes or branches, and the same disordered: the barke somewhat plaine, and not very rugged: the leaues be broad, more long than round, and finely nicked in the edges. The flowers are whitish tending to a blush colour. The fruite or Apples do differ in greatnes, forme, colour and taste; some couered with a red skin, others yellowe or greene, varying infinitely according to the soyle and climate; some very great, some little, and many of a middle sort; some are sweete of taste, or something sower; most be of a middle taste betweene sweete and sower, the which to distinguish I thinke it impossible; notwithstanding I heare of one that intendeth to write a peculiar volume of Apples, and the vse of them; yet when he hath done that he can do, he hath done nothing touching their seuerall kindes to distinguish them. This that hath beene saide, shall suffice for our historie.

3 *Malum*

I also hope you may be inspired to grow some of these apples yourself, and so the final part of the book provides some next-step pointers. It includes brief biographies of a few apples that, for one reason or another, were not included in the *Pomona* but cannot be overlooked; a short guide to choosing and caring for your trees; and suggestions of where you can talk to experts, and taste and buy some of these wonderful fruits for yourself.

An apple by any other name

In 'the olden days', apples had generalized descriptive names – the rough-skinned russets and leathercoats, the pip-grown pippins. Large, irregularly round apples were often called catsheads, while costard, from which cats-head may have derived, typically indicated large, ribbed fruits but was often simply a synonym for apple – it also gave us the word 'costermonger' for one who sells fruit and vegetables from a barrow.

Some names have been around for hundreds of years, and attached themselves to many different apples. Codlin/Codling we have already met; Nonpareil and Nonsuch were obviously reserved for apples of particularly fine quality, as was Beefing (if it derives from *beaufin*; but see Striped Beefing, *page 180*). Apples with an angular shape that gave them 'corners' were often called Quoining, which evolved into Queening, while Juneating and its many variations (Joaneting, Jennetting, Gineting and so on) denoted early ripeners that were ready for harvest around St John's Day in June. Pearmain is associated with pear-shaped apples, although it has been given several alternative origins, including *permanus*, relating to long-keeping qualities, or 'from Parma', or *par main*, 'in the hand' – that is, an apple to eat raw rather than prepared in a dessert or pudding. Reinette came over from France, but was so ubiquitous that it doesn't seem to indicate any particular characteristic except perhaps 'queen among apples'. Though even 'little queen' is a disputed translation of *reinette*, as etymologists also reason it might have evolved from *renatus* (rebirth) or *rainette* (little frog, in reference to a slightly amphibious-looking skin). Take your pick.

As we acquired distinguishing surnames, so apples acquired epithets: Worcester Pearmain, Keswick Codlin, Parker's Pippin. An apple's name might change over time or geography; identical apples could be given different local names, and early records were incomplete, unreliable or simply non-existent. Much is being done to sort out points of confusion, but even a brief visit to the informative website of the National Fruit Collection (*see page 242*) will reveal mind-boggling lists of synonyms, both foreign and English, which often run to dozens of names for a single variety.

To say that identifying and correctly naming apple varieties opens a can of worms would be an understatement. To take just one example, this is how Bernwode Fruit Trees (*see page 243*) begin their description of Winter Colman:

> Probably a Norfolk apple and also called Winter Coleman, Norfolk Coleman, Norfolk Storing and Black Jack… It has been confused with Norfolk Beefing and the accession in the National Fruit Trials turned out to be Norfolk Beefing, so the last time Winter Colman was known to be in Britain was 1885, in the *Herefordshire Pomona*.

Mislabelling, disagreements about identity and alternative names abound, so if you have set your heart on a particular variety it is worth doing some homework to ensure you acquire the tree you intend.

For the most part, though, names are a source of enjoyment in themselves. Who could not warm to an apple called Sops-in-Wine or Summer Strawberry, wonder at the exoticism of D'Arcy Spice and enjoy the blunt imagery of Bloody Ploughman? The namers of Kentish Fillbasket and Lady's Delight obviously had an eye on market appeal; Greasy Jack and Carrion possibly less so. You never know where browsing a fruit catalogue or wandering through an orchard may lead, just by name alone. My own eye picked out Duck's Bill simply because I've always had a fondness for ducks, so I was delighted to discover that it was also part of my local horticultural history. May your own explorations lead you down similarly satisfactory avenues.

Information in the apple profiles

NAMES As will be apparent from the preceding pages, history, locality and preference all conspire to ensure that heritage apples seldom answer to one name. Where variants are notable – or notably confusing – this is clarified in the text, but numerous small variations frequently occur (such as Adam's, Adams, Adams's, or between *du* and *de* in French names), and so the names used are the official accession name set by the National Fruit Collection (*see page 242*), rather than conforming entirely with the *Pomona*'s own labelling.

USES Don't take these as exclusive – experiment! 'Cooking apples' is a purely British concept, evolved from the demand for fluffy, acidic apples that lend themselves to traditional pies and puddings. In France and elsewhere, where apples are more commonly used for open tarts that require slices that keep their shape, an apple may be considered *also* good for cooking, but not solely grown or promoted for that purpose.

HARVEST AND STORAGE Timing will vary from year to year and from place to place, so these are broad indications for comparative purposes.

FLOWERING TIME Again, timing fluctuates with location and conditions, often quite widely, but most varieties come to flowering peak within a few days of one another. These are allocated a 'middle-of-the-road' 0. Those which blossom later are indicated by +1 or +2; those earlier by –1 or –2. The importance of flowering time for pollination is explained on page 221, with an accompanying table of FLOWERING & POLLINATION TIMES (*pages 216–18*).

FERTILITY, VIGOUR, FRUIT BEARING AND DISEASES The practical section at the back of the book explains more about each of these aspects of apple-growing, but there are no cut-and-dried degrees of, say, disease resistance or vigour, as so much depends on growing conditions and variables such as the weather.

The apples

Adams's Pearmain

'Pearmain', which appears in a number of apple names, dates back to medieval times and is usually associated with apples that have a pear-like shape (*see page 14*). Unlike pears, when hanging on the tree these apples are wider at the top than at the bottom, so the effect is more heart-shaped. With Adams's Pearmain this is emphasized by the warm red flush the skin takes on when it ripens.

Adams's Pearmain rightly has many fans, who enthuse over its nutty, rich flavour and sweet aroma. Its skin can become a little tough with keeping, but the taste remains, and indeed intensifies over time. The flavour has been compared with a good Cox's Orange Pippin or Egremont Russet (*see pages 56 & 204*), though its less heavy russeting and attractive shape probably give it higher points than an Egremont in the looks stakes.

Little is known about Mr Robert Adams, after whom the apple is named, except that in 1826 he presented samples to the Horticultural Society of London (which became the Royal Horticultural Society, the RHS, in 1862). His pearmain remains a worthy heritage apple, and is a good tree to train as an espalier. However, despite its lovely, showy blossom and good cropping, it has proved an unreliable pollinator of other trees.

INTRODUCED	Norfolk or Herefordshire, before 1826
USES	eating
HARVEST	early/mid-October
KEEPING	until March
FLOWERING TIME	–1
FERTILITY	self-sterile
VIGOUR	small, spreading
FRUIT BEARING	partially tip-bearing; some biennial tendency
DISEASE RESISTANCE	scab-resistant

Alexander

The Alexander in question is Alexander I, Emperor of All Russia (1801–25), and this tree is often labelled 'Emperor Alexander'.

This magnificent apple, certainly fit for an imperial table, was first brought to the notice of British growers in 1805, when Lee & Kennedy of Hammersmith Nurseries sent a specimen to the Horticultural Society of London, noting that the circumference of a typical example was 16 inches (40 cm). It had been received from Riga, on the Baltic coast, having travelled from 'the southern provinces', probably Ukraine. It was said that the Emperor of Russia was sent a consignment of the fruit as a gift each year.

Its great girth made Alexander a popular choice for exhibition growing, and its flesh is pleasantly perfumed and not tart – its primary designation as a culinary apple is mostly due to its size rather than its acidity. Very large fruit can often be blown off a tree prematurely in windy weather, and training Alexander as an espalier has the double advantage of providing a sheltering wall and showing off the eye-catching rosy beauty of the apples to best effect. (But *see page 226* for training, as Alexander has a tendency towards tip-bearing, and heavy pruning can take off the fruit buds.)

INTRODUCED	from Ukraine, *c.* 1805
USES	cooking/eating
HARVEST	mid-September
KEEPING	September–October
FLOWERING TIME	0
FERTILITY	self-sterile
VIGOUR	vigorous
FRUIT BEARING	partially tip-bearing
DISEASE RESISTANCE	partial resistance to mildew, scab

Allen's Everlasting

Not quite everlasting, but certainly a prodigious keeper. Allen's Everlasting
will be ready to pick in October, but if the weather is not too inclement
it will keep well on the tree and continue to improve. Once picked and
carefully stored, the fruit will still be good for several months – they have
been known to last until June.

Allen's Everlasting – who Allen was has not, unlike his apple, survived
the passage of time – was recorded in the Rivers nursery in Hertfordshire
in 1864, but had been grown in Ireland before that. It soon became a great
favourite for its memorable taste as well as its keeping qualities. Its flesh is
firm and slightly dry, with a strong, appealing tartness; the acidity fades
with age, but the strength does not, so it remains a characterful apple even
after long storage.

The visual appearance of all apples can vary a certain amount,
depending on the weather and the location, but this one is more of a
chameleon than most. It can look very similar to the portrait here: darkish
green with a heavy flush to its thick, often russeted skin. But it can also be
smoother, greener, more golden, stripier...

As Allen's Everlasting is a naturally small tree, you may consider a
medium or even semi-vigorous rootstock, because this normally resilient
tree can be troubled with scab on a dwarfing rootstock, and also develop
biennial-fruiting tendencies.

INTRODUCED	from Ireland, 1864
USES	eating
HARVEST	mid-October
KEEPING	until late spring
FLOWERING TIME	o
FERTILITY	self-sterile
VIGOUR	small-growing
FRUIT BEARING	spur-bearing
DISEASE RESISTANCE	good (but see note re scab)

Annie Elizabeth

In March 1917 *Garden* magazine carried a letter headed 'Apple Annie Elizabeth', which began:

> About the year 1866 a Mr. Gretoreux [*sic*], a solicitor of this town, brought for our inspection and opinion a dish of a seedling Apple which he stated he had raised from seed from a fruit of Blenheim Orange....

The writer was John Harrison, of the long-established nurseries in Leicester, and his quiet account of the origins of a then well-known apple, complete with grainy photograph of Mr and Mrs Greatorex proudly posing beside the tree in their garden, must have evoked for readers a happier era before the horrors of world war. His letter recalls that Mr Greatorex named the apple after his daughter, who had died as a young child. Pleasingly, the original tree lives on.

Annie Elizabeth remained a popular commercial variety until the 1930s, and is still a worthy garden apple, especially in colder or wetter areas; it seems to shrug off the usual ills that can beset apple trees. Its strongly vertical habit means it is best grown as a standard.

Much is often made of the blossom, sometimes described as maroon, but, although it is indeed beautiful, it is only the buds that are deep pink; once open they present to the world a more typical light flush, deeper on the reverse. The large apples that follow are particularly good for baking – sweet enough not to need added sugar, and firm enough not to collapse.

Annie Elizabeth (top left)

INTRODUCED	Leicestershire, 1860s
USES	cooking
HARVEST	late October–November
KEEPING	until late spring, with care
FLOWERING TIME	+1
FERTILITY	partially self-fertile
VIGOUR	vigorous, vertical
FRUIT BEARING	spur-bearing
DISEASE RESISTANCE	good; resistant to mildew, scab and canker

Api

A dainty of the apple world, Api was often called the Lady Apple, because she was small enough to carry in a reticule or pocket without bulging. But this lady punches above her weight. She may be no larger than a plum, but is full of fresh juiciness and an intense, aromatic flavour that does not fade with keeping. She also fruits prodigiously all along her branches, the tiny glowing fruit giving the effect of Christmas decoration. Indeed the Victorians used Api in copious quantities for table swags and wreaths, and she was a favourite for including in still-life paintings.

The Api arrived from France in the latter part of the seventeenth century, and had been known for at least a century before that. The name is believed to originate from the Forêt d'Apis in Brittany. The forest hasn't existed for centuries, but French schoolchildren still sing the nursery rhyme: 'Pomme de Reinette et Pomme d'Api…'

Her prettiness and delicacy make this a popular variety for training as a stepover or as a miniature standard in a large pot (*see page 225* for the variety of shapes into which apple trees can be trained). You may also come across other varieties in the 'Api' family, such as Api Rose, Api Noir (a deep purple) and Api Etoile or Étoilé, which has a star-shaped cross-section.

INTRODUCED	from France, 1600s
USES	eating
HARVEST	mid-October
KEEPING	until March
FLOWERING TIME	o
FERTILITY	self-sterile
VIGOUR	small
FRUIT BEARING	spur-bearing
DISEASE RESISTANCE	generally good

Ashmead's Kernel

A modest apple that may not be much to look at, but the dull exterior, often sandpapery with russet, conceals a marvellous complexity of flavours. It is juicy, both sharp and sweet, and with an aroma that hints at something intangibly not quite apple; it is often likened to pear drops, but this unfairly suggests a chemical, boiled-sweet tang. Like many apples of sophisticated flavours, Ashmead's Kernel evolves as it matures, so an apple picked off the tree in October can taste very different from one left on the branch until December, and different again from one stored for a couple of months.

It is usually claimed that a Dr Ashmead raised this variety in Gloucester in about 1700. However, further researches, in particular by the Gloucestershire Orchard Trust, reveal a muddling of similar names – a not unusual occurrence in history – and many conflicting views as to the origins of the apple. The favourite theory now is that it originated in the garden of a Mr William Ashmead in or near Gloucester's Clarence Street.

The status of this old variety has waxed and waned over its 300-year history. It didn't gain real acclaim until the middle of the nineteenth century, then its popularity faltered during the first half of the twentieth century, but in 1981 it finally received a First Class Certificate from the RHS and is now once again an apple lover's favourite.

INTRODUCED	Gloucester, early eighteenth century
USES	eating/cider-making
HARVEST	October
KEEPING	until February
FLOWERING TIME	0/+1
FERTILITY	self-sterile – triploid
VIGOUR	slow to mature, can be an intermittent cropper
FRUIT BEARING	spur-bearing
DISEASE RESISTANCE	resistant to scab and mildew; susceptible to bitter pit

Beauty of Kent

This beauty makes a buxom tree, producing showy, rosy blossom and, from its early years, a heavy crop of good-sized fruit, earning it an Award of Merit from the RHS in 1901. The apples keep their shape when baked and store well. Although primarily a cooking apple, you will often find Beauty of Kent described as 'dual purpose', as its acidity fades to an appealing sweetness with storage.

Beauty of Kent was not widely known before the tail end of the eighteenth century but throughout the nineteenth it was a sought-after winter variety. The *Pomona* claims that it is 'probably the Rambour Franc of the French pomologists', who described it as early as the mid-sixteenth century, although the National Fruit Collection does not connect the two. The name 'Rambour' was given to a number of large, red apples, several of which are still popular in the United States. There the name has evolved into 'Rambo'... and, yes, there is a connection between the apple and how the warrior star of the silver screen got his name. Apparently writer David Morrell was trying to come up for a name for the hero of his first book when his wife came back from shopping with... a bag of Rambo apples. The rest, as they say, is history!

INTRODUCED	Kent, late eighteenth century
USES	cooking; also eating (after storage)
HARVEST	late September–early October
KEEPING	until January
FLOWERING TIME	o
FERTILITY	self-sterile – triploid
VIGOUR	moderate
FRUIT BEARING	spur-bearing
DISEASE RESISTANCE	generally good

Bedfordshire Foundling

When Bedfordshire Foundling appeared on the market in the early nineteenth century it was soon adopted by an enthusiastic following. The esteemed nurseryman and writer Hugh Ronalds described it in his *Pyrus Malus Brentfordiensis* (1831) as 'firm, sweet and juicy; it bakes excellently, and is a very valuable sort', while the 1836 edition of the *Agricultural and Horticultural Gleaner* recommended in its Pomological Notes:

> for training against walls in cottage gardens … the proper sorts are Ribston pippins, Old nonpareils and, if a large kitchen apple be required, the Bedfordshire foundling … where the Ribston Pippin may not succeed, the Bedfordshire foundling will be a hardier substitute….

(The *Gleaner* was the go-to periodical for all things horticultural; articles in the same edition ranged from 'Spade husbandry' to 'Original Remarks on the effect of light and electricity in connection with the phenomena of vegetation'.)

Those who grow it today equally value Bedfordshire Foundling for its generous size and abundance (it is very free-spurring, so inclines to heavy cropping), its ability to fight off scab and mildew, and its rich, mellow taste. It has a very pleasing balance of sweetness and tartness, and the creamy flesh stays firm when cooked, deepening to a straw yellow. It can also be used for juicing and for cider.

Miss Ellis's sample opposite was probably picked a little early, as the Foundling ripens to a pale yellow. Despite its supposed origins in Bedfordshire it is also sometimes referred to as Cambridge Pippin.

INTRODUCED	Bedfordshire, *c.* 1800
USES	cooking
HARVEST	early October
KEEPING	until December
FLOWERING TIME	0
FERTILITY	self-sterile
VIGOUR	moderate
FRUIT BEARING	spur-bearing
DISEASE RESISTANCE	good

Bess Pool

The young woman immortalized by this apple was, by all accounts, a Nottinghamshire innkeeper's daughter who discovered a wild tree laden with enticing rosy red fruit in a local wood. (One can only suppose that they were not suffering from the pockmarked skin depicted here!) Bess Pool's good reputation spread, and about a century later Pearson's, a well-regarded local nursery responsible for a number of apple introductions, propagated more trees from the original and introduced it to the wider world.

The flesh is sweet and well-flavoured, inclined to be dry rather than juicy, and can be used in cooking as well as for eating fresh.

A disadvantage of Bess Pool is that she is inclined to take her time about coming to fruiting maturity, and can be slightly erratic even once she has. On the other hand, a useful attribute is that her pink blossom appears very late in the season, making her a good choice for gardens that get caught by late frosts. The same is true of New Bess Pool, an even more brilliantly flushed and slightly squatter daughter, who appeared on the market about twenty years later.

Bess Pool and New Bess Pool (front)

INTRODUCED	Nottinghamshire, 1820s
USES	eating
HARVEST	early October
KEEPING	until March
FLOWERING TIME	+2
FERTILITY	self-sterile
VIGOUR	vigorous
FRUIT BEARING	partially tip-bearing
DISEASE RESISTANCE	generally good

Betty Geeson

From its introduction in the middle of the nineteenth century (purportedly by a Mr Davies from Pershore, deep in Worcestershire orchard country) Betty Geeson was widely grown for the market right across the Midlands. Its popularity was eclipsed by the greater commercial viability of rivals such as Newton Wonder and Bramley's Seedling (*see page 40*) and it has now become rather rare.

This apple remains, however, a choice cooker, quite sweet although with plenty of acidity to give it a good cooked flavour; it also keeps its shape. Robert Hogg included it among his 'Best Kitchen Apples' in *The Fruit Manual* (first published 1860 and still in print), and in more recent times Nigel Slater has recommended it for open tarts. Trees usually carry abundant crops but can be slow growers, so this is not one for too dwarfing a rootstock (*see page 223*).

And who was Betty Geeson? She is described in the *Pomona* as 'an old woman who lived in a village near Belvoir' and who raised the apple from a pip. She is also credited with sowing the pip that grew into Barnack Beauty (a variety raised in the 1840s near Stamford, only 30 miles or so from Belvoir). So, although Worcestershire claims Betty Geeson as its own, she may be an apple with origins 100 miles away the other side of the Midlands.

INTRODUCED	Worcestershire?, 1854
USES	cooking
HARVEST	late September
KEEPING	until January
FLOWERING TIME	o
FERTILITY	self-sterile
VIGOUR	moderate
FRUIT BEARING	spur-bearing
DISEASE RESISTANCE	average

Blenheim Orange

This celebrated apple was originally named after George Kempster, who around 1740 found a sapling growing against the boundary wall of Blenheim Palace, the immensely grand house that had been completed not long before for John Churchill, Duke of Marlborough and hero of the Battle of Blenheim. The many qualities of 'Kempster's Pippin' soon became apparent and it was widely propagated locally. In 1804 the 4th Duke granted permission for the apple to be renamed Blenheim Orange.

What, then, were these many merits? The fruit has a distinctive sweet, nutty flavour, and is a favourite with cheese. It also maintains its shape when cooked and the flesh, which is firm rather than juicy, has the advantage of not discolouring quickly when cut. The colour, like the flavour, becomes richer as it matures.

The tree is a slow developer, but it is hardy and long-lived, and can grow to a great size, so unless you have plenty of space this is one that would be best kept in rein on a dwarfing rootstock (*see page 223*). Once in full swing it's a tremendous cropper – thin fruitlets ruthlessly to discourage a biennial rhythm – and best as a standard rather than constrained into a cordon or espalier.

The Blenheim Orange's antecedents may be unrecorded, but it has parented a number of good apples, including Annie Elizabeth (*see page 24*) and that giant cooker Howgate Wonder.

INTRODUCED	Oxfordshire, *c.* 1740
USES	cooking/eating
HARVEST	late September, but leave on tree for extra flavour
KEEPING	until December
FLOWERING TIME	0
FERTILITY	self-sterile – triploid
VIGOUR	large but slow-growing
FRUIT BEARING	partially tip-bearing; biennial tendency
DISEASE RESISTANCE	resistant to mildew; some susceptibility to scab

Bramley's Seedling

On the wall of a house in Church Street, Southwell, a plaque declares:

> The Bramley Apple Tree was grown from a pip by a young lady, Mary Anne Brailsford between 1809 & 1815. It was thought it came from an apple grown on a tree at the bottom of her garden (now No. 75). One seedling produced very fine apples in 1837 when the new occupier was Mr. Matthew Bramley. A local gardener, Henry Merryweather, later obtained permission to take cuttings from the tree and it was duly registered as the Bramley Seedling.

Southwell, a historic Nottinghamshire market town, holds an annual Bramley Apple Festival. A stained glass window in its Minster commemorates the bicentenary of the original tree, which still stands (just about). Sadly, for a tree that began life while Napoleon was still waging war across Europe, honey fungus has infiltrated its system.

The Bramley is to cooking what the Cox (*see page 56*) is to eating – not necessarily the best, but by far the best known: sales outstrip all other culinary apples put together. The strapping great trees usually need a dwarfing rootstock to rein them in (*see page 223*), and they produce fruit in prodigious quantities. The apples cook down to a light, tangy fluff much acclaimed as the perfect pie filling.

A surprise, if you have only seen plain green shop-bought specimens, is the rusty-rose flush of a ripe Bramley, but there is available a more brilliantly coloured sport (a naturally occuring variation), Crimson Bramley, which arose in Southwell in 1913.

INTRODUCED	Nottinghamshire, *c.* 1860s
USES	cooking; also juicing, cider-making
HARVEST	mid-October
KEEPING	until March
FLOWERING TIME	0
FERTILITY	self-sterile – triploid
VIGOUR	very vigorous
FRUIT BEARING	partially tip-bearing; biennial tendency
DISEASE RESISTANCE	susceptible to bitter pit; mildew- and scab-resistant

Calville Blanc d'Hiver

The Calvilles are an ancient apple family from France (Calleville in apple-growing Normandy is often quoted as the source for the name). What they share are their prominent lumpy ribbed outline and their pre-eminence as cookers that maintain their shape: the apple par excellence for *tarte tatin* and *tarte aux pommes*.

In theory, different Calvilles abound – in her *New Book of Apples*, the apple bible, Joan Morgan lists no fewer than fourteen – but there is much disagreement over which variety is masquerading under which name. Of those pictured in the *Pomona* the only one generally available is Calville Blanc d'Hiver. It is also among the oldest, recorded in 1628 (perhaps even earlier under a different name). It is not much of a looker: rough-skinned, smallish for a cooker and often lopsidedly bumpy, and it demands warmth and sun. French growers recommend it for the dry, sun-baked slopes of the Pyrenees. But in a good year the aroma is a promise of what is to come. The pronounced fruitiness of the flavour becomes even more intense after a month or so in storage, and by midwinter the apples are sweet enough to eat raw.

Other Calvilles are occasionally obtainable, but Blanc d'Hiver gets the *chapeau*. Robert Hogg dismissed Rouge d'Automne (1851), for example, as 'of inferior quality', but to be fair his sample may not have benefited from a continental summer – or have been a different Calville altogether, such is the entanglement of names.

Calville Blanc d'Hiver and Calville Rouge d'Automne

INTRODUCED	France, late sixteenth/early seventeenth century
USES	cooking/eating; also cider- and vinegar-making
HARVEST	mid–late October
KEEPING	until March
FLOWERING TIME	o
FERTILITY	self-sterile
VIGOUR	small, spreading
FRUIT BEARING	spur-bearing
DISEASE RESISTANCE	scab-resistant

Catshead

Like many old British varieties, this large cooker acquired a name that was bluntly descriptive, and when seen on the tree rather than displayed on a plate its angular shape and the puckering of its base do hint at a cat's whiskered face peering out from the foliage. Another of its monickers, Pig's Snout, may take a little more imagination to see. Or, more prosaically, 'catshead' may just be a corruption of 'costard', one of our oldest varieties now lost to cultivation.

Although not quite as ancient as the fabled costard, Catshead was known by the 1600s and perhaps earlier. It is a classic all-round cooking apple: juicy and tart, with firm white flesh that cooks to a good-flavoured purée, but which when sliced keeps its shape quite well. The thickish and slightly greasy skin helps it store well, ready for wintertime dumplings or baked apples. Several well-regarded later cookers probably have Catshead in their ancestry, including Peasgood's Nonsuch and Lord Derby (*see pages 156 & 130*).

The trees usually crop heavily and benefit from thinning the fruit while they are still small to ensure the remaining apples reach their optimum size (*see page 232*). Reports of disease resistance vary, partly accounted for by growing conditions, but the checkered history of nomenclature in the past indicates that trees identified as Catshead may come from a number of different strains.

INTRODUCED	by early seventeenth century
USES	cooking
HARVEST	early October
KEEPING	until January
FLOWERING TIME	0
FERTILITY	self-sterile – triploid
VIGOUR	moderate, spreading
FRUIT BEARING	spur-bearing
DISEASE RESISTANCE	scab-resistant (*but see left*)

45

Cellini

Many acclamations have over the years commended the distinctive
flavour of Cellini. But our taste perceptions are individual, and it is not
for everyone. Edward Bunyard, the noted early-twentieth-century epicure
who inherited the eminent fruit nursery his grandfather had begun in 1796,
lauded the reliability of Cellini's regular cropping but wrote dismissively
of its taste: 'the curious flavour appeals to some'. The flavour has been
described as 'aniseed-like', 'balsamic', even as having 'liquorice overtones'.
Your own taste buds will decide. Once cooked, the purée is pleasant but
much blander.

   Whatever the views of its 'different' taste, Cellini proved a popular apple
when it was introduced by Leonard Phillips in his nursery at Vauxhall,
South London. One of its parents is believed to have been Nonsuch.
Throughout the nineteenth century it was grown in many of the market
gardens and nurseries that surrounded the capital. In the old kitchen garden
of Marble Hill House, on the banks of the Thames, the Environment
Trust has re-created a Model Market Garden, where Cellini is one of
the chosen heritage apple varieties. And in Lambeth, practically on the
doorstep of the site of Leonard Phillips's nursery, the charity Roots and
Shoots has established a small orchard named after and featuring the local
Cellini apple.

INTRODUCED	London, *c.* 1828
USES	eating/cooking
HARVEST	mid-September
KEEPING	until November
FLOWERING TIME	0
FERTILITY	self-sterile
VIGOUR	moderate
FRUIT BEARING	spur-bearing, heavy cropper
DISEASE RESISTANCE	generally good

Cornish Aromatic

Red, ribbed and russety, that's Cornish Aromatic. Its fruit are often attractively freckled or netted and, being quite late to ripen, the tree provides a beautiful sight in autumn sunshine.

In a good year this apple lives up to its aromatic name, when the crisp, quite dry flesh is rewardingly spicy and flavoursome with overtones which could be described as pear drop or even pineapple – even a hint of brandy? However, it can disappoint after a poor summer. Despite developing fruit-bearing spurs freely, it's not a prolific bearer, but it does crop reliably. And, being born and bred in the West Country, it is a good choice for damper regions. It's a very suitable variety for training as a cordon or espalier – or even a more fancifully ambitious shape to show off its distinctively ribbed fruit (*see page 225*).

Although records show it was 'officially' introduced in 1813, it is known to have been grown in its native Cornwall for perhaps as long as 300 years before that. At some point in its long history it was also known picturesquely as 'Sweet Lark'. That it remains quite widely available today is a testament to its enduring popularity.

INTRODUCED	Cornwall, before 1813
USES	eating
HARVEST	mid-/late October, later if weather permits
KEEPING	until February
FLOWERING TIME	+1
FERTILITY	self-sterile
VIGOUR	vigorous
FRUIT BEARING	spur-bearing
DISEASE RESISTANCE	resistant to canker and scab

Cornish Gilliflower

Its prominent ribbing earned this Cornish native the alternative name of 'Calville d'Angleterre' – just one more addition to the confused Calville scene (*page 42*). It shares with the French Calvilles, and with the more ancient and more eye-catching Cornish Aromatic (*page 48*), the potential when given the right conditions for intense aromatic complexity of taste. Its spicy floral notes are perfectly captured by its name, which it shares with the sweetly scented wallflower (*Erisymum cheiri*). Gilliflower derives from the Middle English for clove, *gilofre* or *girofle*; Latin similarly gave the French their name for the spice and hence for wallflower, *giroflée*.

Sir Christopher Hawkins of Trewithen, a Cornish MP and prominent landowner (he could, he apparently claimed, 'ride from one side of Cornwall to the other without setting hoof on another man's soil'), introduced both Cornish Gilliflower (found in a Truro garden) and Cornish Aromatic to the Horticultural Society of London in 1813.

Gilliflower shares several other features with Aromatic: perfume, love of warmth, light crops – this is not a choice for a cold region or in the expectation of heavy crops. Importantly in this last regard, it is a tip-bearer. Since most of its fruit develops at the end of its stems, it is not an apple to consider as an espalier or cordon.

INTRODUCED	Cornwall, *c.* 1800
USES	eating
HARVEST	mid-October
KEEPING	to February, March with luck
FLOWERING TIME	0
FERTILITY	self-sterile
VIGOUR	moderate, leggy
FRUIT BEARING	partially tip-bearing
DISEASE RESISTANCE	scab-resistant; some resistance to canker

Court of Wick

Flavour is where Court of Wick scores 10 out of 10. Its taste has been described as 'rich and fruity', 'essence of apple', even 'very apple-flavoured', which may seem self-evident but is a reminder of how insipid many of the standard supermarket varieties are.

While its rich, fruity taste is a given, views on its looks are more varied. In the eighteenth-century *Survey Somersetshire* it is described as 'a beautiful variety … in shape, colour, and flavour it has not its superior', but others are less complimentary about its assorted blotches and russeting. Its undercolour can vary from clear gold (one of its parents is reputed to be Golden Pippin; *see page 88*) to dull yellow, but can be overlaid with anything from a few orange streaks to rich sunset shades, depending on the position, the weather and even the soil. Fruit left on the tree until October, and which have benefited from plenty of sun, will be much more highly coloured than those harvested earlier after a poor summer. Fruits are on the small side, but crisp and very juicy; they are sometimes used for cider-making.

Court of Wick was introduced to the market around 1790 by Wood of Huntingdon – an alternative name is Wood's Huntingdon – but it was known even earlier than that, and its name indicates that it was first raised at Court of Wick in north Somerset. Despite its origins in the comparatively mild south-west, this is a very hardy variety, recommended for cold, windy areas.

INTRODUCED	Somerset, 1790
USES	eating
HARVEST	late September
KEEPING	until December
FLOWERING TIME	0/+1
FERTILITY	self-sterile
VIGOUR	vigorous; recommended for training as espalier or cordon
FRUIT BEARING	spur-bearing
DISEASE RESISTANCE	resistant to scab and canker

Court Pendu Plat

This is one of the oldest varieties still regularly available – which speaks volumes for its durability and adaptability. There are claims that the Romans might have introduced it, or possibly the Normans; we are unlikely to know for sure, but certainly by Elizabethan times its popularity was well established.

Court Pendu has many virtues: beautiful white blossom, a compact habit, free-spurring and a great taste. Like many russets the fruit are firm rather than juicy, and pleasingly sweet but with an acidic bite. The flavour improves even further after a short time in store.

The odd name relates to two features: *court pendu* referring to the shortness of the stalk, and *plat* to its squatness – these smallish apples are about half as broad again as they are high. It has accumulated many names over time, some simply corruptions of the original French (Courpandu, Corpandy), others as varied as Woolaton Pippin, Garnon's Apple (probably after the house of the gentleman who introduced the variety to Herefordshire) and Wise Apple.

This last is believed to have arisen because the trees are 'wise' enough to delay blossoming until all frosts have past. However, such late flowering also means potential problems with cross-pollination. See POLLINATION (*page 221*) for tips on overcoming this.

INTRODUCED	France, by 1600s
USES	eating
HARVEST	mid-October
KEEPING	at least to February, with care to April
FLOWERING TIME	+2
FERTILITY	self-sterile
VIGOUR	quite small and slow-growing
FRUIT BEARING	spur-bearing
DISEASE RESISTANCE	some resistance to mildew, canker; good scab resistance (leaves may show signs, but unlikely to spread to the fruit)

Cox's Orange Pippin

In innumerable polls, Cox's Orange Pippin is voted top apple. It is the quintessential apple: a handy size, neat and round, attractively flushed, just a touch of russeting. Then, a bite into the firm, juicy flesh releases a marvellous complexity of flavours that have left enthusiasts reaching into the realm of wine-tasting for giddy adjectives and comparisons.

But. The Cox is not perfect. Early growers worried because they had no effective guard against all the diseases and pests to which the Cox is so prone. Twentieth-century fungicides and pesticides brought it back to favourite apple status, but a Cox is not easy to grow well, either commercially or in the garden. It doesn't like the cold or the wet, it can disappoint if not pruned carefully, or if the fruit are picked too soon (it's worth remembering the old tip: shake it to see if you can hear the pips rattle). Moreover, the name can mislead: not every apple labelled Cox has the attributes of the original (*but see* Cox's Pomona, *overleaf*).

For around 150 years, fruit breeders have been seeking the magic formula for an apple with the taste of a Cox but without its health problems. The search goes on: Mr Cox's apple has a list of progeny that makes Queen Victoria's family tree look sparse. When Richard Cox chanced upon this seedling in 1825, he cannot have known what a worldwide winner he had discovered.

INTRODUCED	1825
USES	eating/cider-making
HARVEST	late September, October if possible
KEEPING	about a month; longer, with care
FLOWERING TIME	0
FERTILITY	self-sterile (although a self-fertile sport was developed in the 1990s)
VIGOUR	moderate
FRUIT BEARING	spur-bearing
DISEASE RESISTANCE	poor

Cox's Pomona

Unlike many apples bearing the Cox name, this is not a sport or hopeful imitation of Cox's Orange Pippin (*previous page*), but a half-sister raised the same year, 1825. They both originated at The Lawns in Colnbrook, the home of Richard Cox (*c.*1766–1845). Cox, a London brewer, had retired to leafy Buckinghamshire (though Colnbrook is now in Berkshire) to plant an orchard. Sadly, although he surely recognized the excellence of the two apples named after him, he never lived to see their fame spread.

Despite probably sharing a parent in Ribston Pippin (*see page 170*), Cox's Pomona is very different from the Orange Pippin, but has great merit of its own. The apples are quite large and rosy, and are truly dual-purpose, equally fine as eaters or cookers. They are juicy and crisp, with an excellent flavour, and are especially good baked.

Cox's Pomona makes a very pretty tree, particularly in the spring, when its prolific blossom develops from shell-pink buds to shining white flowers. It is also less fussy than the Orange Pippin, more amenable to cooler regions (it has long been a favourite in Scandinavia since being introduced there in the 1870s) and is a reliable cropper.

INTRODUCED	Buckinghamshire, 1825
USES	cooking/eating
HARVEST	mid-September
KEEPING	until December
FLOWERING TIME	0/+1
FERTILITY	self-sterile
VIGOUR	moderate
FRUIT BEARING	spur-bearing
DISEASE RESISTANCE	good

D'Arcy Spice

A hero from a Regency romance, surely, or perhaps a girlie pop star? But no, an apple, and not even a prepossessing one. D'Arcy Spice acquired its name from the Essex village of Tolleshunt d'Arcy. For many years (but sadly no longer) a row of the trees lined the entrance to the moated Elizabethan Hall where the original tree was found in the eighteenth century. However, the apple is still enthusiastically grown in many village gardens – not for its looks, but for its local ties and, especially, its unusual flavour.

This is a very late variety, quite sharp-tasting when it is first picked. Traditionally it is harvested on 5 November, Bonfire Night, but not eaten until the following March. It is as the apples mature that the 'Spice' element in the name comes to the fore. As long as the fruit have had a good, hot baking in the sun before being picked, the initial tartness develops into a very distinctive nutmeg-like flavour. After a poor summer, it must be said, the flavour can evolve into nothing more than a disappointing mustiness. Moreover, this is not the most reliable cropper every year.

On the plus side, however, D'Arcy Spice is a hardy variety, tolerant of a wide range of conditions, and the showy blossom stands up well to frost. It is a slow grower that never gets very large even on a semi-vigorous rootstock – see ROOTSTOCKS, *page 223*, for more information.

INTRODUCED	Essex, 1785
USES	eating
HARVEST	October/November
KEEPING	with care, until May
FLOWERING TIME	0/+1
FERTILITY	self-sterile
VIGOUR	weak to medium
FRUIT BEARING	partially tip-bearing
DISEASE RESISTANCE	good resistance to mildew and bitter pit; some resistance to canker and scab

Devonshire Quarrenden

Despite its name, this small, handsome apple is believed to have been raised in France before making its way across the Channel, but it was known here by 1678. One of the possible explanations for its name is that it originally came from the medieval Normandy town of Carentan, in the heart of northern France's orchard country. In another mash-up of its name, it was frequently called the Quarantine Apple in Victorian times.

With its deep scarlet colouring and bright, flavoursome flesh, Devonshire Quarrenden enjoyed a long period of popularity all through the nineteenth century. Its taste has been likened to strawberries (though some people detect a metallic tang). With beauty and fine flavour on its side, the only downside is that it doesn't keep; indeed, the fruit has a tendency to fall early. Pick by the end of August and eat as soon as possible, ideally straight from the tree, as within a week or two its crisp, juicy flesh will have become woolly and flaccid.

This is not a vigorous tree, but it is hardy and grows well in the north as well as the warmer, wetter south-west where it achieved its greatest popularity. It was one of the parents of Worcester Pearmain (*see page 194*), to which it passed on its brilliant colouring and, sometimes, its strawberry sweetness.

INTRODUCED	mid–late seventeenth century
USES	eating; also for juice
HARVEST	mid- to late August
KEEPING	eat fresh
FLOWERING TIME	−1
FERTILITY	partially self fertile
VIGOUR	small, weak, with a spreading canopy
FRUIT BEARING	spur-bearing; biennial tendency
DISEASE RESISTANCE	scab-resistant

Duchess of Oldenburg

The string of names that this apple has attracted – Borovitsky (under which name it appears in the *Pomona*), Borovinka, Charlamowsky, Dombrowski, Harlamovoskoe among others – is an indication of its journey in the course of the eighteenth century across Scandinavia and Germany from Russia. Not long after arriving in Britain it was renamed again, possibly after a sister of Tsar Alexander I, who has his own apple named after him (*see page 20*).

The beautiful Duchess has proved a tough survivor. A couple of decades after its arrival in Britain it was chosen as one of the four 'pioneer' Russian varieties sent to Massachusetts to test its hardiness. It passed with flying colours and is still a popular heirloom apple in the USA, and grandparent of an American favourite, Honeycrisp.

The fruit are real beauties: large, round, smooth-skinned and strongly striped red over a pale green base that matures to pale gold. They can be eaten fresh, if you like your apples tart (and they have a habit of falling before they are fully ripe, when they are even sharper), but their forte is as a culinary apple, producing a refreshing, juicy purée. Although the apples do not keep for long, Duchess of Oldenburg is an immensely hardy tree that will survive, indeed thrive and fruit rewardingly, in the worst of climates.

INTRODUCED	*c.* 1817
USES	cooking; also eating
HARVEST	mid-August
KEEPING	about a month
FLOWERING TIME	−2/−1
FERTILITY	self-sterile
VIGOUR	medium
FRUIT BEARING	spur-bearing
DISEASE RESISTANCE	scab-resistant

Duchess's Favourite

The ranks of the aristocracy are quite well represented in the apple world. This duchess was Frederica, Duchess of York, a daughter-in-law of George III. She lived, separately from her husband, at Oatlands Park, Surrey, just a couple of miles from the renowned nurseries of John Cree at Addlestone. Cree counted among his customers the Duke of York's grandmother, providing plants for the fledgling horticultural gardens at Kew. It is said that the apple's delightful rosiness caught the duchess's eye, and hence the name. Cree's *Hortus Addlestonensis* (1829), published nearly a decade after the duchess's death and listing 111 apples, simply called it Duchess of York's. Whether John Cree decreed it or not, Duchess's Favourite is how it is now known to the world.

A nice snippet of history, then, for a very pretty little fruit, and Duchess's Favourite went on to become a popular variety among market gardeners around London throughout the nineteenth century. It would probably not figure in the top rank of heritage apples, but is nevertheless a pleasing apple, especially when you slice it open and discover a pink flush to the flesh too. It doesn't make too large a tree, is a reliable cropper, and when well grown the apples can develop an appetizing hint of strawberry.

INTRODUCED	Surrey, *c.* 1800
USES	eating
HARVEST	early September
KEEPING	eat fresh
FLOWERING TIME	0
FERTILITY	self sterile
VIGOUR	medium
FRUIT BEARING	spur-bearing
DISEASE RESISTANCE	generally good

Duck's Bill

It takes a stretch of the imagination to see the similarities between this apple and a duck's beak, but it does have a slightly scooped profile; so if you get just the right apple at just the right angle…

This Sussex variety is always linked with Fred Streeter, the amiable 'voice of gardening' on the BBC for forty years (some may still remember his rich country burr broadcasting from the original TV garden on the slopes of Alexandra Palace). Streeter was head gardener at Petworth House in West Sussex, and it was from there that he sent samples of his Duck's Bill to the National Fruit Trials in 1937. There is some question as to whether these pre-war apples were identical to the old cottage favourite grown for centuries in Sussex, but it would be nice to think so.

There is a pleasing sweetness/acidity to the full-flavoured, dense, crisp flesh, and although it is often labelled primarily an eating apple it might be justly considered dual-purpose – it cooks well, keeping its shape rather than melting down to a froth, and is sweet enough not to need added sugar.

Duck's Bill can be variable in its growth and fruiting, though, and even on its native South Downs its performance can disappoint, putting on wood at the expense of fruit.

INTRODUCED	unknown
USES	eating/cooking
HARVEST	early October
KEEPING	until December
FLOWERING TIME	+1
FERTILITY	self-sterile
VIGOUR	vigorous
FRUIT BEARING	spur-bearing
DISEASE RESISTANCE	generally good

Dumelow's Seedling

Until the arrival on the market of the ubiquitous Bramley (*see page 40*), this was one of the premier culinary apples available to nineteenth-century cooks. It was – and still is – prized for its rich sharp flavour and fine creamy texture, ideal for apple sauce and for baking, and also valued for its keeping qualities. The very beautiful pink blossom is another outstanding feature.

It has collected a number of name changes in its life since it was raised by a Leicestershire farmer, Richard Dumelow (or Dumeller, pronounced Dumelow) at the end of the eighteenth century. London horticulturalists were introduced to it in 1818 as Dumelow's Crab, but its name was changed to Wellington a year or two later, in honour of the victorious Duke. It later reverted to commemorate our (by then deceased) Leicestershire farmer and its official name is now Dumelow's Seedling. But it is widely known, particularly in the north, as Normanton Wonder and also still sold under the name Wellington (a name now bestowed on a different apple, so do check you're getting the variety you want).

This fine old variety may have been overshadowed by Bramley, but it remains a good alternative to consider, especially in a colder region. It also sired another heritage favourite: Lane's Prince Albert (*see page 120*). It develops spurs freely, which means it's a good cropper – in most years the young fruit will need thinning out to encourage apples of a decent size and discourage a biennial tendency.

INTRODUCED	Leicestershire, 1700s
USES	cooking
HARVEST	mid-October
KEEPING	to March, or later with care
FLOWERING TIME	+1
FERTILITY	self-sterile
VIGOUR	moderate, spreading
FRUIT BEARING	spur-bearing; slight biennial tendency
DISEASE RESISTANCE	slightly susceptible to scab (but doesn't render fruit inedible)

Early Julyan

In common with many dual-purpose apples, Early Julyans are sharp rather than sweet, but in a good way: not mouth-puckering but refreshing and lively, what those who grow and taste apples professionally often call 'brisk'. As a cooker they produce a golden purée with a light, fruity taste.

This is not a variety that is widely available, but it is worth seeking out, particularly if you have an interest in traditional Scottish apples. It is sometimes marketed as Tam Montgomery, especially north of the border. The trees are quite hardy, and reliable and prolific in their fruiting. Although the apples can develop a rosy flush on their sun-facing side, they are ready once they become pale yellow, and because they ripen as early as July they can catch you on the hop and fall from the tree before you even realize they are ready to pick.

The highly respected nurseryman and pomologist Hugh Ronalds introduced Early Julyan to the English market via his nursery in Brentford, Essex, in about 1800, but it had been grown and enjoyed in Scotland long before that.

INTRODUCED	Scotland, before 1800
USES	cooking/eating
HARVEST	July–August
KEEPING	no
FLOWERING TIME	−1
FERTILITY	self-sterile
VIGOUR	vigorous
FRUIT BEARING	spur-bearing
DISEASE RESISTANCE	average

Ecklinville

Ecklinville is one of Ireland's notable heritage apples. Its name recalls the
estate on which it was grown (now more usually written Echlinville), on the
Ards Peninsula, east of Belfast. Ecklinville was being widely grown by 1800
and was treasured as a culinary apple – the 1883 National Apple Congress
included it in their best dozen varieties for cooking. But, as was the fate
of many other varieties, demand for it dropped once fruit and vegetables
began to be transported any distance, because it bruises easily and became
unprofitable commercially.

For the average garden or allotment, however, Ecklinville has plenty to
offer. It's a lovely looking tree, growing naturally into a pleasing shape, and
puts on a wonderful show of blossom in the spring. It also fruits reliably and
usually prolifically. The apples themselves, typically a good large cooker
size, can be very varied in their colouring. Depending on how they are
grown and the amount of sun, the bright green skin may mature to a clear
yellow or retain its greenness but gain a red flush on the sun-ripened side.
Either way, the flesh is fresh and sharp and cooks down to a well-flavoured
purée, which the Victorians prized, as we should, for apple sauce.

INTRODUCED	Northern Ireland, by 1800
USES	cooking; occasionally used in cider-making
HARVEST	early September
KEEPING	until November
FLOWERING TIME	0
FERTILITY	self-sterile
VIGOUR	vigorous
FRUIT BEARING	spur-bearing
DISEASE RESISTANCE	scab-resistant

Fearn's Pippin

John Rogers, who styled himself 'Nurseryman formerly of the Royal Gardens', wrote in 1834 in praise of Fearn's Pippin's colour and flavour, and also that its strong short stalk 'enables the fruit to remain fast to the branches, when many others are thrown to the ground by the winds'. 'The original tree of this variety first seen by the author', he rather pompously noted, 'belonged to a person of the name of Bagley at Fulham.'

The Bagleys were long-established market gardeners in what was then on the western outskirts of London; they were known as the 'Kings of Fulham'. Bagley's Lane still winds most of the distance between New King's Road and the Thames. Robert Bagley, or possibly his father Richard, is credited with having introduced this pretty apple in the latter part of the eighteenth century; it became widely planted in the home counties for the London market. Its high colouring – often more brightly scarlet than shown here – and its fine, sweet-acidic, fruity taste found favour all through the following century, and yet it is now rarely grown, despite being a sturdy tree that produces crisp, juicy fruit that taste as good as they look.

INTRODUCED	London, *c.* 1780
USES	eating; sometimes used for cooking
HARVEST	early October
KEEPING	until January
FLOWERING TIME	−1
FERTILITY	self-sterile
VIGOUR	medium
FRUIT BEARING	spur-bearing
DISEASE RESISTANCE	generally good

Forge

Forge was 'the cottager's friend', a hard-working tree that provided prolific crops of juicy, tasty apples that could be eaten fresh yet were sharp enough to cook with, or could be pressed for cider or stored for a good part of the winter. Although it was first noted in 1851, Forge was growing well before that in many gardens and orchards in the Weald, which extends across East Sussex, southern Surrey and western Kent. Its rather un-fruity name derives from the fact that it comes from the heart of what, from pre-Roman times until the nineteenth century, had been south-east England's iron-working region; it shared the landscape with ancient hammer ponds and pre-industrial forges, particularly in the East Grinstead area.

Today, Forge is still found around the Weald, not on a commercial scale but flourishing in gardens and community orchards. It is appreciated for the numerous good-looking, colourful apples it reliably produces every year, which can either be eaten straight away, if your taste buds favour the sharp, or stored until they mellow to a softer, sweeter version. Cooked, the fruit melt to a soft, fruity purée that makes an excellent apple sauce.

INTRODUCED	East Sussex, before 1851
USES	eating/cooking/cider-making
HARVEST	late September
KEEPING	at least December
FLOWERING TIME	+1
FERTILITY	self-sterile
VIGOUR	moderate
FRUIT BEARING	spur-bearing
DISEASE RESISTANCE	very scab-resistant

Gladstone

Gladstone the politician: born 1809, declared prime minister for the first time 1868. Gladstone the apple: 'born' around 1780, reintroduced 1868, renamed (Mr) Gladstone 1883.

Back in Gladstone's day, the apple named after him would have been welcomed as one of the first of the season, and we should still enjoy it straight from the tree as soon as it is ready. It is a charming example of what might be called an 'old-fashioned apple': sweet and perfumed, with a lack of invigorating bite. To catch it at its best, allow it to ripen but not over-ripen, as its raspberry-like freshness too soon descends into a soft woolliness. Trees usually carry a heavy crop, but keep a lookout for fruit that have split.

It was a Kidderminster nurseryman, William Jackson, who rediscovered the original tree (then estimated to be about a hundred years old, but still flourishing) and it was known in the market as Jackson's Seedling for the next fifteen years, until it was lauded at the 1883 National Apple Congress, awarded a First Class Certificate and renamed after the prime minister (by then the Grand Old Man of British politics). Its popularity spread beyond its native Worcestershire and it was a well-known variety right up until the 1960s.

INTRODUCED	Worcestershire, *c.* 1780
USES	eating
HARVEST	late July
KEEPING	eat fresh
FLOWERING TIME	0
FERTILITY	partially self-fertile
VIGOUR	quite vigorous, spreading
FRUIT BEARING	partially tip-bearing; can sometimes become biennial
DISEASE RESISTANCE	resistant to canker and scab

Gloria Mundi

An apple called 'Glory of the World', with alternative names that include Mammoth, Ox Apple and Monstrous Pippin, is never going to get over-looked! A specimen submitted from Illinois to the *American Agriculturist* in 1860 had a recorded circumference of 18 in. (46 cm) and weighed in at 3½ lb (almost 1.6 kg). (As is the way of challenges, the Illinois mammoth has long been outstripped, with the current record – but for how long? – held by a Japanese giant weighing in at 1.859 kg or just over 4 lb.)

But as a horticultural periodical of the era commented:

> Although it is gratifying to the amateur to be able to produce such extra large specimens, it is not, we think, to be regretted that they are not common … at what a risk should we walk in the orchard – a blow from the falling of such a meteor would be no light casualty! … The great improvement being made in the flavor of this standard fruit is a matter for far greater satisfaction than it would be to produce such monstrosities.

The Gloria Mundi is not without merit – its large blossoms are beautiful and the cooked flesh melts down to a mild golden purée – but it is a horti-cultural rather than a culinary glory. It continues to be more popular across the Atlantic.

See also Mère de Ménage (*page 144*), which is also sometimes erroneously sold under the name Gloria Mundi.

INTRODUCED	USA 1804, possibly earlier in Germany; to UK 1817
USES	cooking
HARVEST	early October
KEEPING	until December
FLOWERING TIME	0
FERTILITY	self-sterile
VIGOUR	moderate
FRUIT BEARING	partially tip-bearing
DISEASE RESISTANCE	very good

Golden Harvey

Although this is appreciated as a deliciously tasty eating apple, Golden Harvey's great reputation is as a cider apple. The heavily russeted old-gold fruits produce a juice so charged with sugars that, once fermented, it results in a cider so strong that it was often given the alternative name Brandy Apple.

The trees themselves are hardy and reach a good size (depending, of course, on their rootstock) and are recommended for training as an espalier, but they are not quick to produce fruit. Individual apples are small, just 5 cm (2 in.) across, but their rich, tangy, aromatic flavour is reward for the wait, and intensifies even further after storage. They keep very well, even into May or June if stored carefully – old gardening books often recommend keeping them in boxes packed with slightly damp sand, a method traditionally also used for root vegetables such as carrots and parsnips, as it kept them frost-free and away from the light, and the sand prevented them from shrivelling.

Golden Harvey should not be confused with the larger Harvey (*see page 98*), and it may still be possible to come across yet other varieties known locally as Harvey. In 1828 the *Pomological Magazine* reported that 'in the cider counties there appear to be three distinct kinds under that name, and the Harvey Apple of Norfolk is a sort totally different from either of these three.'

INTRODUCED	Herefordshire, seventeenth century
USES	cider-making/eating
HARVEST	mid-October
KEEPING	until March
FLOWERING TIME	o
FERTILITY	self-sterile
VIGOUR	large
FRUIT BEARING	spur-bearing
DISEASE RESISTANCE	slightly susceptible to scab

Golden Noble

A fine culinary apple that should be better known – Golden Noble is often a good alternative to the classic Bramley's Seedling (*see page 40*) for a garden tree. It has a more graceful habit of growth, requires only one pollinator not two, and produces an excellent-flavoured purée that requires less sugar than its more famous, tarter cousin. The blossom is especially attractive, too, usually missing the late frosts and quickly losing its early pink flush to delight with a showy cloud of pure white. The RHS gave it the coveted Award of Garden Merit in 1993.

Golden Noble is credited with arriving on the scene in 1820. This is when Patrick Flanagan, head gardener at Stow Hall, south of King's Lynn, submitted examples for exhibition at the Horticultural Society of London, and it came to wider notice. However, the orchard in which his Golden Nobles were picked was already old, certainly dating back to when the gardens of the second Stow Hall (built in 1796 to replace an earlier ruined Hall) were laid out at the end of the eighteenth century. Stow Hall itself does not survive, but the gardens are a focal point of the village, especially for the Apple Day festivities held each October.

INTRODUCED	Norfolk, 1820
USES	cooking/cider-making
HARVEST	early October
KEEPING	until December, with care all through the winter
FLOWERING TIME	+1
FERTILITY	self-sterile
VIGOUR	moderate
FRUIT BEARING	partially tip-bearing
DISEASE RESISTANCE	resistant to canker, scab, mildew

Golden Pippin

Small, sweet, rich and lemony: Golden Pippin makes a delightful, if tiny, eating apple, but was once also popular in the kitchen for pippin jelly, or poached whole and presented at table as perfect little golden globes.

Golden Pippin has been a popular descriptive name for a number of apples over the centuries. The one available today may not be the variety described by the early botanist John Parkinson in 1629, but it is believed to have originated at one of the great Elizabethan manor houses of Sussex: Parham Park. Popular throughout the nineteenth century, it then all but disappeared from the market. The *Pomona* recounts one explanation circulating at the time: that Covent Garden Market supplies, where it was selling for 4–5 shillings a bushel, had been bought up in their entirety for the Empress of Russia at a guinea (21 shillings) a bushel!

It is more likely that its size came to tell against it commercially, but its genetic potential had already been recognized. Thomas Andrew Knight used Golden Pippin in his first breeding programmes in the early 1800s, and in time it was outstripped by many of its progeny, several of which – including Court of Wick, Pitmaston Pine Apple and Yellow Ingestrie – feature in this book.

This little apple has also been immortalized in a different way: as a not-so-minor character in Tracy Chevalier's 2016 novel *At the Edge of the Orchard*.

INTRODUCED	probably Sussex, early eighteenth century
USES	eating
HARVEST	early October
KEEPING	until January or sometimes later
FLOWERING TIME	o
FERTILITY	self-sterile
VIGOUR	moderate
FRUIT BEARING	spur-bearing
DISEASE RESISTANCE	scab-resistant

Golden Spire

Golden Spire doesn't grow very tall, and so its graceful, slightly weeping habit and highly decorative blossom make it a lovely tree for the smaller garden. It is a hardy variety that produces lots of fruiting spurs and plentiful crops – you may need to be assiduous with your thinning (*see page 232*) to give individual fruits a chance to grow to a decent size. As a further plus, its sunny yellow, distinctly oval apples can be described as triple-purpose.

While classed first as a fine culinary apple, it is also considered a good cider variety, expressing copious amounts of well-flavoured, astringent juice. Although it was first found growing in Lancashire, its discoverer, Richard Smith, was a Worcester man, so no doubt – Worcestershire being a traditional cider county – he was quickly alert to the cider-making potential of his new find. In Gloucestershire it was primarily grown for cider and was known (and sometimes still is) as Tom Matthews.

The apples can also make good eating, when the cidery flavour comes through even fresh from the tree, but wait until they are fully ripe or you may just get a mouthful of rather watery, underpowered flesh. Cooked, they melt down to a tasty but tart yellow purée that may be too sharp for most palates without the addition of some sugar or honey.

INTRODUCED	Lancashire, *c.* 1850
USES	cooking/cider-making; also eating
HARVEST	early September
KEEPING	about a month
FLOWERING TIME	−1
FERTILITY	self-sterile
VIGOUR	small, weeping
FRUIT BEARING	spur-bearing
DISEASE RESISTANCE	good

Gravenstein

The gourmet Edward Bunyard wrote of the Gravenstein in 1937: 'No apple has a more individual flavour; alas, that its cropping powers are so small!' It is not widely known or easily available today, perhaps because it is rather a betwixt and between. Its size and irregular shape argue against it as a first-class eater, while it doesn't quite have enough acidity for a perfect cooker. But it makes a decent fist of both, and is excellent for juicing. The distinctive flavour, sharp and almost savoury under the sweetness, makes Gravenstein one worth seeking out to see if it suits your palate.

Despite Bunyard's comment, it is a good cropper, but only after some years, and the fruit drop easily. As they tend to ripen over a long period it provides an extended harvest of a few apples at a time, making it better suited to a garden than commercial production. A bonus is the very large white flowers – they have even been likened to a wild rose.

The Gravenstein may have originated in southern Denmark/northern Germany or gravitated there in the seventeenth century from the Italian alps. Soon after its arrival in Britain, around 1820, it was sent to New England and Nova Scotia to see if it thrived in harsher climates (it did). About the same time Russian settlers were planting it on the west coast of America – remnants of once-huge orchards still remain around Sebastopol, California – and nowadays it is better known in the USA and Canada.

INTRODUCED	via Denmark, mid-seventeenth century
USES	eating; sometimes also cooking
HARVEST	early September
KEEPING	until end October
FLOWERING TIME	−2
FERTILITY	self-sterile – triploid
VIGOUR	vigorous
FRUIT BEARING	partially tip-bearing
DISEASE RESISTANCE	slightly susceptible to scab

Grenadier

If Bramleys (*see page 40*) weren't around, Grenadiers would probably be everyone's cooking apple of choice. Indeed, before being upstaged by the greater keeping qualities of the Bramley it was the most commonly grown cooking apple in commercial orchards. The crisp green apples make a lovely creamy purée with a perfect balance of sharpness and honey.

It is sometimes said that the best-tasting apples are the most difficult to grow, with awkward growth habits or martyrs to every passing pest or disease. But Grenadier is such an amenable tree: a good grower even in wet regions but without being over-vigorous, and it reliably produces heavy crops of juicy fruit early in the season. It has proved a fertile pollinator of other trees and is largely untroubled by the usual diseases that plague so many other varieties; just watch out for capsid bugs, which it seems to attract.

Grenadier attracted plaudits at the National Apple Congress in 1883, while still quite a new kid on the block – it had been an unknown before being exhibited by Charles Turner twenty years earlier. It was described as 'first quality; a very fine and handsome apple' and the Congress report said of George Bunyard's samples (he had submitted 120 different varieties from Kent): 'The examples of Grenadier were specially noteworthy and were awarded a First Class Certificate.' It still holds the RHS Award of Garden Merit.

INTRODUCED	Buckinghamshire, *c.* 1862
USES	cooking
HARVEST	mid-August
KEEPING	until end September
FLOWERING TIME	0
FERTILITY	partially self-fertile
VIGOUR	medium
FRUIT BEARING	partially tip-bearing
DISEASE RESISTANCE	good; resistant to scab, canker and mildew

Hanwell Souring

Hanwell Souring is named not after a West London district under the Heathrow flight path, but after a hamlet in Oxfordshire, just north of Banbury. It is believed to have been raised there at the beginning of the nineteenth century.

The Souring part of the name is self-explanatory – this is not an apple to sample straight off the tree if you don't want your taste buds to go into shock! But this acidity is just what makes it a good cooker, when the crisp white flesh reduces down to a still sharp but fruity purée. It was also traditionally valued as a cider apple. The nineteenth-century apple expert Robert Hogg called Hanwell Souring 'a first rate kitchen apple'. It was popular all through the Victorian era and for another twenty years or so until, like many another, it faltered under the inexorable rise of the Bramley.

Once widely grown all over Oxfordshire and the West Midlands, it is now difficult to find, although it survives in a few old orchards (and no doubt some gardens, quite possibly unidentified), and the RHS Gardens at Wisley in Surrey have several specimens. It is a distinctly upright tree, with none of the rounded or spreading habit of most varieties.

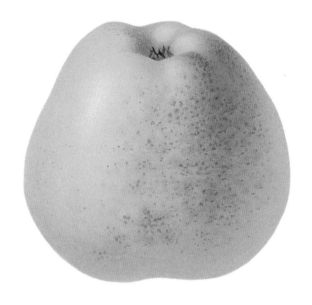

INTRODUCED	Oxfordshire, 1820
USES	cooking; also cider-making
HARVEST	mid-October
KEEPING	until January
FLOWERING TIME	0
FERTILITY	self-sterile – triploid
VIGOUR	tall, upright
FRUIT BEARING	spur-bearing
DISEASE RESISTANCE	good

Harvey

Not the most handsome of apples, admittedly, with its irregular shape and the somewhat patchy russeting that forms like a net over its skin, but Harvey's many fans appreciate what lies within: firm, aromatic, sweet-citrussy flesh which cooks to a beautiful rich purée. It bakes well and has been described as the perfect apple for mincemeat. It also consistently rewards with heavy crops of large fruit that, with care, can be kept through Christmas, by which time its natural sweetness has developed, the firm flesh has softened and the apples can be eaten raw.

Harvey is a very old variety – Charles I's botanist John Parkinson mentioned it in his *Paradisi in Sole Paradisus Terrestris* (1629) – but history seems to have distorted the source of its name. It is often labelled Dr Harvey, supposedly after Dr Gabriel Harvey, a seventeenth-century master of Trinity Hall Cambridge. However, this appears to conflate two different gentlemen, both called Harvey, both hailing from East Anglia and both associated with Trinity Hall. The controversial literary figure Gabriel (not Dr) Harvey was indeed a fellow at Trinity Hall, and longed to be its master but never succeeded. The year he petitioned for the post coincided with the death of a former master of Trinity, Dr Henry Harvey, which may be where the confusion has arisen. And, should you wonder, Golden Harvey is a different apple altogether (*see page 84*).

INTRODUCED	pre-1629
USES	cooking
HARVEST	mid-September
KEEPING	until November or into December
FLOWERING TIME	0
FERTILITY	self-sterile
VIGOUR	medium
FRUIT BEARING	partially tip-bearing
DISEASE RESISTANCE	slightly susceptible to scab

99

Hawthornden

When Hawthornden's fine, pale golden skin becomes touched by the late summer sun it becomes a blushing beauty. But this delicacy can be easily bruised, contributing to its fall from favour by the twentieth century, when mass transport demanded robuster varieties.

Hawthornden was introduced to London kitchens at the end of the eighteenth century but had been known and grown long before that in its native Scotland – its name comes from a village in the rolling countryside of Midlothian, south of Edinburgh.

The *Pomona* says categorically that Hawthornden is 'suitable only for kitchen use', but it is sometimes recommended as an eating apple too, if it is left on the tree long enough to sweeten. However, it is as a cooker that it comes into its own, producing gently flavoured tarts or puddings, and it is excellent as a large baked apple.

Being a northern variety, it stands up well to cold conditions, and it produces prolifically. John Lindley described in his *Pomologia Britannica* (1841) how 'as the extreme buds of the branches are mostly blossom-buds, the ends become pendulous when the crop of fruit is fully grown.'

INTRODUCED	Scotland, 1780
USES	cooking
HARVEST	mid-September
KEEPING	until November or December
FLOWERING TIME	0
FERTILITY	self-sterile
VIGOUR	moderate, spreading
FRUIT BEARING	spur-bearing
DISEASE RESISTANCE	susceptible to mildew

Herefordshire Beefing

Herefordshire Beefing is not large for a cooking apple, and very different in character from the pale fluffiness of the esteemed early Lord Suffield or Peasgood's Nonsuch (*see pages 132 & 156*), or the old codlins. When baked or roasted the dense flesh becomes rich and soft but retains its shape, which made this and the Norfolk Beefing popular for drying (*see page 152*). When reduced to a purée, the flesh retains its excellent flavour and deepens in colour to a beautiful rich yellow.

The blossom puts on a great show in the spring, typically followed by a rewarding crop (the flowers are usually late enough to avoid damage by all but exceptionally late frosts), but you'll need to keep an eye on the trees as harvesting time draws near: the fruit do tend to drop before you expect.

This is an apple that has been around since the eighteenth century, but referred to as just Beefing. When Robert Hogg sampled it at the Woolhope Naturalists Club show in 1876 (the Introduction tells the story of the club and *The Herefordshire Pomona*) he believed it needed distinguishing from the Norfolk Beefing… but then discovered that the same 'Herefordshire' differentiation had been suggested seventy-five years earlier but never officially recorded. The case of an apple so good they named it twice?

INTRODUCED	Herefordshire, 1700s
USES	cooking/eating; also drying
HARVEST	early October
KEEPING	until December
FLOWERING TIME	+1
FERTILITY	self-sterile
VIGOUR	medium
FRUIT BEARING	tip-bearing
DISEASE RESISTANCE	good

Irish Peach

While it is undeniably satisfying to slice open an apple in the depths of winter, to have its scent and taste bring back the memories of autumn harvest, this is not what Irish Peach offers. This apple is all about instant gratification, the pleasure of biting into a sun-warmed apple straight from the tree. Irish Peach is soft (don't expect a crunch), aromatic and lusciously sweet, but these qualities have to be enjoyed in the moment; they will not wait around. Not only will the fruit not keep in storage, they are keen to drop from the tree as soon as they can.

Irish Peach arrived at the Horticultural Society of London in 1819, sent by a Kilkenny nurseryman by the name of John Robertson, but the apple is believed to have been developed on the other side of Ireland, around Sligo. It was popular as a dessert apple at the Victorian dinner table throughout the nineteenth century, but, as faster and more reliable transport services were developed, Irish Peach lost out to other, longer-keeping varieties that became available.

However, a shortcoming such as lack of shelf life is no disadvantage in a home-grown tree, and more than offset by Irish Peach's beautiful pink-flushed blossom and fresh-tasting early fruit.

INTRODUCED	Ireland, *c.* 1820
USES	eating/cider-making
HARVEST	end July/August
KEEPING	no
FLOWERING TIME	–1
FERTILITY	self-sterile
VIGOUR	vigorous
FRUIT BEARING	tip-bearing
DISEASE RESISTANCE	some resistance to mildew and bitter pit

Kentish Fillbasket

It's probably stating the obvious to say that this is a large apple and that it originated in Kent! From the early nineteenth century it was grown in many Kentish orchards and was in the vanguard of apple trees exported to Australia to kick-start the apple-growing industry there. Ironically, it is now easier to find in Antipodean nurseries, especially in New Zealand. However, there are a few stockists 'back home', and it is often among the varieties chosen for the increasing number of community orchards being planted in the southern fringes of London, helping both to 'green the grey' and to reclaim tiny parcels of historic Kent that have been swallowed up by the suburbs of the capital.

In its heyday Kentish Fillbasket was rated as a good, strong-growing tree that bore an abundant crop of first-class culinary apples, whose sharp, faintly green-tinted flesh was admirably suited for sauce or baking – and these are the reasons to grow it today.

A little slice of local history, then, and worth seeking out, especially if you live in the area that was once proud to be the Garden of England.

INTRODUCED	Kent, by 1820
USES	cooking
HARVEST	mid-October
KEEPING	until January
FLOWERING TIME	0/−1
FERTILITY	self-sterile – triploid
VIGOUR	vigorous
FRUIT BEARING	spur-bearing
DISEASE RESISTANCE	good

Kerry Pippin

A Kerry Pippin's skin is a first indication of its special appeal: glossy mottled orange and gold, often partly overlaid by a delicate tracery of russet. Bite into that pretty skin and you'll first enjoy a satisfying crunch – unlike many early-season apples it is not in the slightest soft – and then are likely to be smitten by the sweet intensity of flavours, highly aromatic and fruity.

As its name implies, this is an Irish heritage apple, first recorded in 1802 by the Kilkenny-based horticulturalist John Robertson. It was soon much in demand far beyond its original home, and the respected botanist John Lindley described it as 'scarcely rivalled, in its season, for high flavour, richness, and beauty'. It soon became a favourite for the Victorian table.

These are small, neat apples and the trees that bear them are also neat and easy to manage, and usually enjoy good health. Kerry Pippin lends itself to training as an espalier or cordon, or a small pyramid. It produces fruit-bearing spurs with great freedom, resulting – barring disastrous weather – in a terrific show of faintly blushing blossom followed by heavy crops of its charming and appetizing fruits.

INTRODUCED	Ireland, 1802; to UK 1819/20
USES	eating
HARVEST	late August–early September
KEEPING	about a month
FLOWERING TIME	–1
FERTILITY	self-sterile
VIGOUR	medium
FRUIT BEARING	spur-bearing
DISEASE RESISTANCE	mildew-resistant; variable resistance to scab

Keswick Codlin

Rather ignominiously, Keswick Codlin's origin has been traced back to a rubbish heap. True, it was on the land of a castle, but Gleaston Castle, on the Furness Peninsula where it juts out into the Irish Sea, has long been a ruin and doesn't lend much glamour to this apple's story.

But the apple itself has much to recommend it, and would be a good choice if you want an amenable tree that will give you early fruit for multiple uses. A Cumbrian nurseryman, John Sander, recognized its value when he introduced it to the public in about 1793, and it became a popular variety for the market gardens around London as well as in northern orchards.

It's a hardy, easy-going tree, with very pretty, fragrant blossom and reliably heavy crops (thin its fruitlets to avoid it overbearing and getting into a biennial pattern). Keswick Codlin can be harvested early – there are records of it being used for pies as early as July. Although it makes a decent sharp eating apple, it is generally considered a cooker. The pale, slightly flushed fruit cooks down to a creamy purée and, when baked or puréed, is sufficiently sweet to need no more than a pinch of sugar. It was especially prized in Victorian times for jelly-making – perfect for mint or rosemary jelly as an appropriate accompaniment to Cumbrian lamb.

INTRODUCED	Lancashire, late eighteenth century
USES	cooking/eating
HARVEST	mid-August
KEEPING	about a month
FLOWERING TIME	−1
FERTILITY	partially self-fertile
VIGOUR	medium, compact
FRUIT BEARING	spur-bearing, some biennial tendency
DISEASE RESISTANCE	good; especially resistant to scab

King of the Pippins

A versatile apple with numerous guises, at various times King of the Pippins has been Hampshire Golden, Jones' Southampton Yellow, Queen of the Pippins, Seek No Further and Shropshire Pippin, among many other names. Its history is also knitted in with the eighteenth-century Reine des Reinettes, and it is now believed to be the same as this prized French apple. The *Pomona* labelled it Golden Winter Pearmain but by the 1870s this older name was already giving way to the snappier King of the Pippins.

Rough russeting can gives the old-gold skin a dull finish, but when fully ripe it takes on a pleasing orange-red flush. The flesh beneath is juicy, sharp yet sweet, with echoes of different fruits – people have detected notes of citrus, strawberry, even banana in spite of a slight bitterness. At the 1883 National Apple Congress it was submitted by a great many of the exhibitors, who voted it first in the Dessert Apple category: it received 98 votes (Cox's Orange Pippin came second with 89, perhaps losing ground not from any lack in flavour but, as the Congress report noted, because King of the Pippins was a better grower in the damper north and west). Despite the juiciness, the flesh is firm rather than crisp, and turns golden with cooking – it's a favourite in France for an open *tarte aux pommes*. The juice also makes good cider.

INTRODUCED	*c.* 1800
USES	cooking/eating; also cider-making
HARVEST	early October
KEEPING	until January or February, with care
FLOWERING TIME	0
FERTILITY	partially self-fertile
VIGOUR	medium
FRUIT BEARING	spur-bearing; some biennial tendency
DISEASE RESISTANCE	good; scab- and mildew-resistant

Kingston Black

Most ciders are a blend of different apple juices, selected to produce a desirable balance of flavours; Kingston Black is one of the few to have sufficient depth and breadth of flavour to make a one-variety cider. It arose in Somerset, probably around Kingston St Mary, just north of Taunton (it is also known as Taunton Black), but the quality and distinctive flavour of the juice encouraged its planting all over the West Country and up into the cider country of Herefordshire and Worcestershire.

Of course, the apples are not truly black, but they do ripen to a deep maroon, often much richer and darker than Edith Bull's painting. Even the cider they produce has a dark hue, suitable for its full-bodied, bitter-sharp style.

The downfall of these prized apples is the health record of the trees that bear them. They take a number of years to reach fruiting maturity and usually don't carry heavy crops once they do. They are also prone to canker and scab, so they will need a sharp eye on them to keep these scourges at bay. This all explains their disappearance from most commercial orchards, but they should be a vintage cider apple with a future among cider connoisseurs with a home apple press.

INTRODUCED	Somerset, 1820s
USES	cider-making
HARVEST	early November
KEEPING	no
FLOWERING TIME	o
FERTILITY	self-sterile
VIGOUR	moderate, spreading
FRUIT BEARING	spur-bearing
DISEASE RESISTANCE	susceptible to canker and scab

Lady Henniker

John Perkins arrived at Thornham Hall, the Suffolk estate of Lord Henniker, as a young gardener in 1848. Before long he had set about raising a new apple variety, beginning the process with a robust scattergun approach. The estate cider house had great quantities of pippy 'must' left over from apple pressings, so his method was to sow barrel-loads of this and watch to see what germinated. He grew on only the most promising, eliminating a few more each year, until he and his lordship agreed on a fine apple that looked good on the table and served well baked or puréed. It was named after the lady of the house and presented to the RHS, who awarded it a First Class Certificate, in 1873.

The trees proved not only to crop reliably and quite prolifically, but to be hardy and easy to grow, and the apples were rewarding: large and rather square, gold flushed or streaked with red and, when cooked to a fluff, maintaining a strong apple flavour and aroma that needed no extra sweetening. Given these qualities it is slightly surprising that Lady Henniker is not more widely grown today. Perhaps it's that the trees are not precocious fruiters, or that the apples are quite variable in shape and colour. But John Perkins saw their visual as well as culinary merits: in 1877 he included them among the recommended fruits in his *Floral Designs for the Table*, the first book on flower arranging by a head gardener.

INTRODUCED	Suffolk, 1873
USES	cooking/eating
HARVEST	late September–early October
KEEPING	until January
FLOWERING TIME	o
FERTILITY	self-sterile – triploid
VIGOUR	vigorous
FRUIT BEARING	spur-bearing
DISEASE RESISTANCE	good

Lamb Abbey Pearmain

Delicious: that's the verdict on this little apple. The juicy, aromatic flesh is packed with zest, with a tang of pineapple among the complex flavours. The trees crop generously and, what's more, the apples keep well, so their sweet intensity can be enjoyed through to the new year and beyond.

The list of medals presented by the Horticultural Society of London in 1818/19 included the following recognition:

> To Mary Anne Malcolm of Lamb Abbey in Kent, for her success in raising seedling Apple trees, fruits of which have been tasted at different Meetings of the Society, and highly approved, particularly that now named the Lamb Abbey Pearmain…

Lamb Abbey is now Lamorbey and absorbed into London's south-east suburbs, but in Mrs Malcolm's day was surrounded by hop fields and orchards. The Malcolms were a prominent local family (their mansion home is today the Rose Bruford College of Theatre and Performance). Mary Anne's most successful apple is believed to have been raised from a pip of Newtown Pippin, one of America's all-time favourite apples and introduced to Britain in the 1760s.

Having been popular all through the nineteenth century, Lamb Abbey Pearmain almost disappeared from the scene, but was rescued from oblivion in the 1940s by the food writer and bon viveur P. Morton Shand. It is now available from a few heritage apple growers, but more widely grown in the USA, perhaps because of its link to the Newtown Pippin.

INTRODUCED	Kent, 1804
USES	eating
HARVEST	late September
KEEPING	until January
FLOWERING TIME	−1
FERTILITY	self-sterile
VIGOUR	moderate
FRUIT BEARING	spur-bearing
DISEASE RESISTANCE	slightly susceptible to scab

Lane's Prince Albert

This flavoursome cooker, sharp but not quite as acidic as a Bramley, is probably a cross between Dumelow's Seedling (*see page 70*) and Russet Nonpareil. It arose in the garden of a Berkhamsted resident, Thomas Squire, who called it Victoria and Albert in honour of a brief visit the queen and her consort paid to the Hertfordshire town in 1841 – some accounts have him actually planting the tree in his front garden as the royal cortège rode by. John Lane, of the renowned local fruit nursery, then acquired grafting stock and in 1857 introduced it to the world as 'Prince Albert'. Appropriately, the walled garden at Osborne House, Victoria and Albert's holiday residence on the Isle of Wight, features a walkway of espaliered Lane's Prince Albert.

It remains a popular apple, producing abundant crops on an attractively shaped tree that never grows too big. The fruit are large and shiny, bright green lightly flushed by the sun. They can bruise easily, so this is a variety that has fallen out of favour with commercial growers, but remains a good garden choice, especially as it thrives in a wide range of soils and conditions and is not a fussy or 'difficult' tree. The apples do mellow enough after a few months in storage to be eaten raw – though still too sharp for many tastes – but their prime role is as excellent bakers or for pies and crumbles.

Lane's Prince Albert (left)

INTRODUCED	1840s
USES	cooking
HARVEST	mid-October
KEEPING	until March
FLOWERING TIME	0
FERTILITY	partially self-fertile
VIGOUR	moderate
FRUIT BEARING	spur-bearing; biennial tendency
DISEASE RESISTANCE	resistant to canker and scab; susceptible to mildew

Lemon Pippin

The Lemon Pippin is certainly about the same size as a large lemon, but after that opinions are divided as to whether it gained its name from the shape, the colour, the aroma or the taste – or all of these. There is a tendency for the king fruit – the larger apple at the centre of a cluster of little apples before they are thinned – sometimes to grow up around the stalk to create a pear/quince/lemon-at-a-stretch shape. The apples do often ripen to a lemon yellow but just as often take on a duller greenish yellow with patches or netting of russet that remove any resemblance to a lemon. And the scent and taste? Definitely citrus notes to its flavour, but a lemon aroma is only detectable by some people some of the time.

A variable, unpredictable apple, then, but nonetheless interesting. Its history is uncertain – it may be English or have come over from France; it may or may not be the same as the ancient Quince Apple (a description that fits it well) – but by the eighteenth century it was in demand in the discerning London market and sought-after for jellies and tarts or for drying to make sweetmeats. Today, although much smaller than a classic culinary apple, it serves all those purposes and is also an interesting, densely textured eating apple.

INTRODUCED	eighteenth century or earlier
USES	eating/cooking
HARVEST	early October
KEEPING	until December, or until spring with care
FLOWERING TIME	+1
FERTILITY	self-sterile
VIGOUR	small to medium
FRUIT BEARING	spur-bearing
DISEASE RESISTANCE	good

Loddington

Presiding over the orchard of Sulgrave Manor, a Tudor manor house not far from Oxford (and, incidentally, home of George Washington's ancestors), is the venerable 'King Lod' tree, still producing good crops of Loddington apples after more than 180 years.

Loddington gets its name from a village in Kent, still in the heart of orchard country, but the story goes that the original was brought there from Bath, by a niece of Mr Robert Stone, who set about propagating it. It is still known as Stone's Loddington, or just Stone's (but not to be mistaken for Stone Pippin). Just to add to the confusion, it is sometimes referred to as Killick's Apple, after Mr Lewis Killick, from the neighbouring village of Langley, who presented the apples to the RHS Fruit Committee in 1877 (which awarded it a First Class Certificate).

After its introduction into the 'Garden of England', Loddington became widely grown in the Home Counties for the London market and was highly regarded as a culinary apple. The tree itself is a strong grower and fruits prolifically – its natural habit is to produce spurs abundantly – and the apples are large, handsome and juicy. Although it is primarily grown for cooking (it melts down to a flavoursome purée), the apples can also be eaten raw once they have mellowed with a little keeping.

INTRODUCED	Kent, 1820
USES	cooking
HARVEST	late September
KEEPING	until December
FLOWERING TIME	o
FERTILITY	self-sterile – triploid
VIGOUR	medium, spreading
FRUIT BEARING	spur-bearing
DISEASE RESISTANCE	average

London Pippin

If this is the 'Lounden Peppen' recorded in a notebook of the 'Trevelyans of Somersetshire', it is a very ancient variety, from before 1580, possibly originating in Essex. Or in Norfolk. But it has a confused history before the 1830s, and is probably synonymous with the Five-Crowned Pippin. This alternative name refers to its angular ribs, which form a distinct ring of prominent peaks around the 'eye' at the apple's base.

Whatever its past and its provenance, this is a variety of more than just historical interest. It makes a good culinary apple, its crisp, sharp flesh keeping its shape as it cooks, but turning golden, rich and sweet, or it can be enjoyed fresh, the acidity not overwhelming the pleasant nuttiness. Although it has a slight tip-bearing tendency it produces spurs freely, and yields abundant crops most years. The large fruit store well, without shrivelling, until the spring.

This was one of the more successful apples introduced to Australia, where it was established as the 'Aussie farmers' apple', and for a while exported back to its native land. It is usually known Down Under as Five-Crowned Pippin, or just Five Crowns, and conserved as an Australian heritage variety.

INTRODUCED	unknown
USES	cooking/eating
HARVEST	mid-October
KEEPING	until March
FLOWERING TIME	+1
FERTILITY	self-sterile
VIGOUR	medium
FRUIT BEARING	mostly spur-bearing
DISEASE RESISTANCE	good

Lord Burghley

Darkly handsome, rich and sweet: that's Lord Burghley the apple, although Lord Burghley the peer and politician, on whose estate the seedling apple tree was found in the 1830s, was certainly rich too – his great-great-granddaughter Angela Cecil Reid has written about the fortune he lavished on yachts, travel, gambling and entertaining.

The great Elizabethan Burghley House, near Stamford, lies in the soft green country where Lincolnshire, Cambridgeshire and Northamptonshire meet. Stamford and the surrounding villages were renowned in the nine-teenth century for their apples (see Betty Geeson's association with Barnack Beauty, *page 36*), and even today at blossom time lone ancient village trees burst into a froth of pink and white, ghostly markers of long-abandoned orchards.

Once Lord Burghley was launched on to the market in 1865 it became a favourite for its looks and taste, but also for its ability to last in the apple store – kept carefully it could provide a family with sweet eating apples until June, closing the gap before the first apples of the new season. Indeed, it is often considered at its best after a month or so in storage. It makes an attractive, spreading tree that crops well, and is an apple that should still be grown for the qualities that the Victorians appreciated in it.

Lord Burghley (right and back)

INTRODUCED	Lincolnshire, 1865
USES	eating
HARVEST	mid-October
KEEPING	until April
FLOWERING TIME	+1
FERTILITY	self-sterile
VIGOUR	moderate, spreading
FRUIT BEARING	spur-bearing
DISEASE RESISTANCE	slightly susceptible to scab

Lord Derby

The Lord Derby was raised in Cheshire, and is marvellously well adapted to the cooler, wetter conditions typical of the north-west. Its hardiness makes it particularly popular in Scotland. The trees themselves are not very large, but reliably produce abundant harvests of strapping great fruit – even with assiduous thinning of fruitlets in June, in a bumper year the branches may need to be propped up to take the weight.

As well as being obliging with its crops, Lord Derby puts on a beautiful show of blossom: pale pink petals opening from rich cerise buds to lovely effect. The apples, bright green mellowing to a greenish yellow, have an angularity that hints at a possible Catshead ancestry (*see page 44*). When cooked they retain an excellent rich, sharp but not over-acidic flavour, and the purée takes on a hint of pink. Storage softens the sharpness, but some of the flavour also leaches away, so although they will keep successfully for two or three months they should be used before all the green has left the skin.

The apple was named after the three-times prime minister, who, perhaps confusingly, did not come from Derby, but took his title from the old Lancashire hundred of West Derby. He was the grandson of the founder of the world-famous Derby horse race.

INTRODUCED	Cheshire, 1862
USES	cooking
HARVEST	late September
KEEPING	until December
FLOWERING TIME	0/+1
FERTILITY	partly self-fertile
VIGOUR	vigorous
FRUIT BEARING	spur-bearing
DISEASE RESISTANCE	resistant to scab, canker and mildew

Lord Suffield

It's easy to see how this apple became such a favourite in Victorian gardens and kitchens: its good-sized fruit appears early in the season and in great profusion, and the juicy, sharp flesh cooks down to a lovely soft fluff. But it is also understandable why it fell out of favour – the trees themselves are not very long lived, and the pale, delicate skin is easily bruised so the apples don't travel well. A good choice for a garden, then, but not for a commercial orchard. Its pale pink blossom is so pretty that it was often recommended as a decorative tree, as crab apples and cherries are frequently used today.

The tree was first bred in 1836–7 by Thomas Thorpe, a weaver from Middleton, near Manchester. He raised his apple on land belonging to Middleton Hall, and named it after the local lord of the manor. Lord Suffield (1734–1810), though a Norfolk man, had inherited the manor of Middleton through his wife and had become a generous benefactor to the growing mill town. Today, he is commemorated with a blue plaque in Long Street and this apple.

INTRODUCED	Manchester, 1836
USES	cooking
HARVEST	mid-August
KEEPING	until September
FLOWERING TIME	−2/−1
FERTILITY	self-sterile
VIGOUR	strong-growing but not over-large
FRUIT BEARING	spur-bearing
DISEASE RESISTANCE	susceptible to canker

Lucombe's Pine

An apple that tastes of pineapple? Once you are alert to the scent and taste association between the two fruits, you may be able to discern it in several varieties, even those that don't flag it up in their name.

Lucombe's Pine is a Devon apple that provides both history and flavour. In 1720 William Lucombe established the first commercial nursery in the West Country, and Lucombe & Pince, later Exeter Nurseries, thrived throughout the eighteenth and nineteenth centuries. Part of the site is now Pince's Gardens, so retaining a horticultural link, though today hemmed in by leafy suburban streets and allotments. The apple that Lucombe's nursery reared here is not very large, with a clear yellow skin freckled with russet sprinkles; it makes an aromatic eating apple and is relished for its delicious juice. It doesn't produce very heavy crops but is a good choice for training as an espalier (*see page 225*).

Still unsure about the pineapple thing? If a 'pineapple' apple variety is out of reach or out of season, you can even detect it in Moroccan or pineapple broom (*Argyrocytisus battandieri*), the large showy shrub with flower clusters that look and smell like miniature pineapples. Sniff the flowers but with apples in your mind, and your nose may experience the equivalent of one of those optical-illusion pictures that can be two things at once.

INTRODUCED	Devon, eighteenth century
USES	eating; also for juicing
HARVEST	early October
KEEPING	until December
FLOWERING TIME	0
FERTILITY	self-sterile
VIGOUR	moderate
FRUIT BEARING	spur-bearing
DISEASE RESISTANCE	very resistant to scab

Manks Codlin

In his *Flora and Pomona* of 1829, Charles McIntosh (who at the time was head gardener to Queen Victoria's uncle, Prince Leopold, at Claremont in Surrey) provided a precise description of the Manks Codlin's origins:

> This excellent culinary apple originated in 1811, from seeds sown by Mr. James Kewley, (well known as the inventor of several ingenious pieces of mechanism applicable to horticultural purposes,) in the garden of his father, Mr. Kewley, of Ballanard, about a mile and a half from Douglas, Isle of Man. It produced two fruit for the first time in 1815.

As you might expect from an apple first raised on a windswept island in the Irish Sea, this is no frail specimen that needs pampering, and is often recommended as a 'good doer' in poor soils and exposed positions. It is not especially vigorous but, as McIntosh reported, it matures precociously, producing fruit when very young. Once established it is a good bearer and the firm, juicy fruit cooks down to a flavoursome fluff.

Although originating from the Isle of Man, the National Fruit Collection's official accession record gives its name as 'Manks' rather than the usual 'Manx' spelling. This is not a widely available variety, so it is worth bearing the alternative spellings in mind when tracking down a source.

INTRODUCED	Isle of Man, 1815
USES	cooking
HARVEST	mid-August
KEEPING	until October
FLOWERING TIME	−1
FERTILITY	self-sterile
VIGOUR	moderate, spreading
FRUIT BEARING	spur-bearing, heavy cropper with biennial tendency
DISEASE RESISTANCE	good

Mannington's Pearmain

Some apples are carefully bred and have a fully recorded family tree; many more – such as this one – are happy accidents of nature. John Mannington was a butcher by trade but also a keen and knowledgeable apple man, and he recognized the potential of one of the trees that had grown up in his grandfather's garden in Uckfield, Sussex. It had germinated, probably some seventy years earlier, from one of the thousands of pips from discarded pomace, the residue after pressing for juice. In 1847 he sent a sample to the Horticultural Society of London, who declared it an excellent dessert variety.

Mannington's apple soon caught on in Victorian homes, and should be more widely grown today. It doesn't make an over-large tree, but when still young produces good crops of juicy, medium-sized fruit with a well-balanced flavour overlaid by a pleasant nuttiness from its russet overcoat. It becomes sweeter and richer in flavour if left on the tree to ripen as long as possible. After that it keeps well and, although it shrinks in storage, retains its good flavour.

INTRODUCED	Sussex, 1847
USES	eating
HARVEST	mid-October
KEEPING	until February
FLOWERING TIME	0
FERTILITY	self-sterile
VIGOUR	moderate
FRUIT BEARING	spur-bearing
DISEASE RESISTANCE	good

Margaret

Another name often given to Margaret is 'Red Joaneting', which, when written as Jun-eating, supposedly hints at when it is ready for harvesting. June may be a little optimistic, but Margaret apples are certainly one of the first on the summer scene, and by about St Margaret's Day on 20 July they will have turned bright scarlet and be ready for picking. In common with most early varieties, they won't keep, but fresh from the tree they are refreshingly juicy, with a bright, sharp taste. Pick them promptly, or they will spoil even on the tree.

Margaret has an upright habit but doesn't grow too large, and it would be a good candidate for a double or single cordon (*see page 225*).

This is an ancient variety. It is mentioned in John Rea's *Flora* (1665), though is probably older, and by the time John Pechey was writing his *English Herbal of Physical Plants* in 1694 its credentials were well established:

> The English Apples being accounted the best in Europe, I will mention particularly those that are most esteem'd amongst us. First, Those that are soon ripe, and soon decay. The Gineting, the Margaret or Magdalene…

Like Rea he gives 'Magdalene' as an alternative name. (This may explain why, with the liturgical calendar featuring rather less in our lives than in the seventeenth century, many sources misattribute St Margaret's Day to St Mary Magdalene's, two days later).

INTRODUCED	seventeenth century
USES	eating
HARVEST	late July
KEEPING	no
FLOWERING TIME	+1
FERTILITY	self-sterile
VIGOUR	small to moderate
FRUIT BEARING	spur-bearing
DISEASE RESISTANCE	slightly susceptible to scab

Margil

There are some once-popular apples that have all but disappeared from our fruit bowls but deserve to make a comeback. Margil is one of them. It is similar in size and looks to a Cox's Orange Pippin (*see page 56*); indeed it has been suggested they may have a common ancestor. It's a beautiful looking apple, streaked with glowing oranges and reds and with an excellent flavour, rich and aromatic, sweet yet tangy.

Margil was introduced more than 250 years ago, probably from France, possibly from Louis XV's Versailles. One of its French names is Reinette Musquée – *reinette* being one of those indeterminate labels for many apples but reserved for what the Victorians called 'the finest sorts', and *musquée* for its perfumed aroma. By 1750 it was well established and continued to be in demand for the table through to the end of the nineteenth century.

The trees are not very strong growers (though they are hardy) and do not reliably bear bounteous crops – some gardeners have found one of its alternative names, Never Fail, to be rather misleading! This may have been the reason for Margil's fall from favour. Despite the *Pomona* declaring 'no garden should be without it', this is probably not one to choose as your single tree, but it would be a delightful addition to a small heritage orchard.

INTRODUCED	before 1750
USES	eating
HARVEST	early October
KEEPING	until December or the new year
FLOWERING TIME	0
FERTILITY	self-sterile
VIGOUR	small to moderate
FRUIT BEARING	spur-bearing
DISEASE RESISTANCE	susceptible to canker; some scab resistance

Mère de Ménage

Picture a cartoon housewife: big, burly, raw-elbowed and red-faced, and then picture the apple version of such a caricature. That's Mère de Ménage ('housewife' in French): large, knobbly and soon reddened by the sun.

This apple has been around for a very long time, since at least the late eighteenth century. Given its name, it probably came over the Channel from the Continent. Belgium is a likely original home, but Denmark has also been mooted. Whatever its origins, it suits the British climate and is very hardy, even in northern or windy areas. The scarlet apples make a great show on the tree.

Mère de Ménage is sometimes recommended as a dual-purpose apple, but, although not as acidic as a Bramley, it is too dry and tart for most palates. Cooked, though, is another matter, when the lack of juice becomes an asset. It is very well suited to pies and puddings such as apple charlotte that require dense chunks of fruit that aren't going to collapse or ooze. The flesh also turns a pretty pink, adding to its appeal in a dessert.

Mère de Ménage (*right*)

INTRODUCED	by 1780
USES	cooking
HARVEST	early October
KEEPING	until February
FLOWERING TIME	0
FERTILITY	self-sterile – triploid
VIGOUR	vigorous
FRUIT BEARING	partially tip-bearing
DISEASE RESISTANCE	good

Minshull Crab

Despite sounding like a Cornish crustacean, Minshull Crab hails from the north-west and is far from being a tiny crab apple. The original tree grew in the pretty little village of Church Minshull, not far from Crewe, and Minshull Crab came onto the market in 1777. It was also known as Lancashire Crab – 'crab' often being used to denote an apple that kept well. Over the following century it was popular throughout the region, especially welcomed by the fast-growing spinning towns around Manchester, nicknamed 'Cottonopolis'. As King Cotton came to dominate the region, former market towns became booming but congested conurbations filled with inhabitants who had no time or space to grow their own food.

Although Minshull Crab is ready for harvesting in October, it is an apple that is best stored for a few weeks after picking, but even then is a very sharp, hard-fleshed cooker; don't expect it to mellow sufficiently to be eaten raw. Not in the top rank, perhaps, but it's a robust, trouble-free tree that will provide useful apples for storage over the winter, and the *Pomona* reported it 'one of the best sauce apples that grows'.

INTRODUCED	Cheshire, mid-eighteenth century
USES	cooking
HARVEST	mid-October
KEEPING	until March
FLOWERING TIME	−1
FERTILITY	self-sterile – triploid
VIGOUR	moderate
FRUIT BEARING	spur-bearing
DISEASE RESISTANCE	slightly susceptible to scab

Mother

Mother lives up to her rosy good looks with a sweet juiciness and a distinctive scent that is part sugar, part spice. At least, that's Mother at her best; in some years she can tip over into rather mushy soft sweetness. Then it's best not to store the apples but to turn them into a pink-flushed purée to enjoy in apple pies.

These are hardy trees and have no problem with cold climates and even poor summers; the pretty blossom is helpfully frost-resistant too. Reports on their cropping are variable – some growers find them bountiful; others unpredictable and light, and not necessarily in a biennial pattern. This may be due to the fact that they are promoted as partly self-fertile: even self-fertile trees crop better if they can be pollinated by other varieties.

A reason for Mother's hardiness is that she was bred in New England, west of Boston. She was introduced to Britain in 1844 by Thomas Rivers of the renowned Sawbridgeworth Nurseries on the Hertfordshire–Essex border – Mother is often called American Mother, perhaps to differentiate her from local varieties such as Sussex Mother. The Rivers family was responsible for introducing several American apples to Britain (as well as the ubiquitous Conference pear), and some fifty years later Mother was in turn the parent of another Rivers-bred apple appropriately named Thomas Rivers. Both remain popular heritage varieties. A 4-acre remnant of the Rivers nurseries is now a carefully conserved heritage orchard.

Mother (*right two*)

INTRODUCED	USA, 1844
USES	eating
HARVEST	late September
KEEPING	until December
FLOWERING TIME	+1
FERTILITY	partially self-fertile
VIGOUR	moderate
FRUIT BEARING	spur-bearing
DISEASE RESISTANCE	resistant to mildew and scab; susceptible to canker

Newland Sack

An apple that comes from the heart of Worcestershire orchard country, an excellent apple with many qualities – yet Newland Sack is now very difficult to find. Often, varieties that were in demand in the nineteenth century lost out to the mass-market demands of the twentieth because they wouldn't keep or they weren't good travellers or they were just too small or light-cropping to be worth growing commercially. None of these shortcomings applies to Newland Sack.

Typically, the trees produce a heavy harvest of good-sized, slightly unsymmetrical but not ugly fruit that colour nicely in the sun. Although primarily a culinary apple, it has stalwart keeping properties and by Christmas has sweetened enough in store to make fine eating. It doesn't bruise easily and – an admirable and unusual asset in an apple – seems not to rot even if it has been bruised.

The original seedling grew up at Newland Court, near Malvern, and gained an enthusiastic following that spread once William Crump exhibited it in London in 1888. (Crump, a well-known figure in the world of Victorian apples, was the head gardener at the adjacent Madresfield Court, which owned Newland Court.) It is a mystery why such a paragon of an apple failed to maintain its standing, but it was completely lost to cultivation until the beginning of this century, when an old tree was identified on the original farm and new budwood grafted by the Marcher Apple Network (*see page 243*). Although saved from total oblivion, it remains a rarity.

INTRODUCED	Worcestershire, *c.* 1800
USES	cooking/eating
HARVEST	October
KEEPING	until May
FLOWERING TIME	0
FERTILITY	self-sterile
VIGOUR	vigorous
FRUIT BEARING	spur-bearing
DISEASE RESISTANCE	good

Norfolk Beefing

Norfolk Biffins, squab and swarthy, setting off the yellow of oranges and lemons … urgently entreating and beseeching to be carried home in paper bags and eaten after dinner.

Charles Dickens, *A Christmas Carol*, 1843

This dark-flushed apple with meaty, acidic flesh that mellows to sweetness with a touch of cinnamon by spring was widely grown and eaten in Dickens's day, and possibly dates back to the seventeenth century. It makes a handsome tree, very beautiful in blossom, hardy and vigorous, with heavy crops most years.

It also gives its name to the biffin, a type of half-preserved apple sweetmeat that was popular up until the Second World War. Apples, left whole and sometimes stuffed with citrus peel, would be coated with sugar and baked for hours in a cool oven with a press over them to flatten them as they cooked. It would take a firm-fleshed, tough-skinned apple for this to work successfully, and Biffins were widely acknowledged to be the best: 'The Norfolk biffin answers for this dish far better than any other kind of apple', wrote Eliza Acton, the Victorians' Delia Smith.

Norfolk Beefing, Norfolk Colman and Winter Colman are all very similar, and in many quarters deemed to be the same.

INTRODUCED	Norfolk, pre-1807
USES	cooking/eating; also drying
HARVEST	mid-October
KEEPING	until March or April
FLOWERING TIME	0
FERTILITY	self-sterile – triploid
VIGOUR	vigorous
FRUIT BEARING	spur-bearing
DISEASE RESISTANCE	resistant to mildew and scab

Oslin

Although the Oslin is recorded as having been introduced in 1815, it is acknowledged to have been around for centuries before that, possibly brought over by French monks. Its spiritual home, if not its origin, is Arbroath, on the east coast of Scotland – you'll come across it referred to as Arbroath Oslin or Arbroath Pippin. Oslins have now once again been planted in the town, close to Applegate, which marks the location of the large orchard that the monks of Arbroath Abbey once tended.

A curiosity of the Oslin is that its branches develop distinctive burrs or knobs – one of its misnomers is Burr Knot – that will send out roots if planted up in late winter, making it one of the very few apples that can be propagated successfully from cuttings.

Being a Scottish apple, the Oslin is hardy and will produce a reliable crop even in cold areas. It's quite a vigorous, upright grower, with a good show of richly pink-flecked blossom. The yellow fruit that follows is crisp and aromatic – some have likened its taste to melon; others have detected an undertone of aniseed.

INTRODUCED	Scotland, before 1815
USES	eating
HARVEST	late August
KEEPING	about a month
FLOWERING TIME	−2
FERTILITY	self-sterile
VIGOUR	moderate
FRUIT BEARING	spur-bearing
DISEASE RESISTANCE	good, but old wood can be prone to canker

Peasgood's Nonsuch

No one knows the exact parentage of Mrs Peasgood's original seedling, but it does indeed deserve its 'nonsuch' epithet. The splendid show of extra-large white blossom is usually followed by a heavy crop of large apples that look magnificent on the tree as the sun ripens them to a green-gold streaked with scarlet.

Although first and foremost a culinary apple, Peasgood's doesn't have the ultra-tartness of some cookers, and is often treated as an eating apple; the Victorians favoured it for the table because of its fine size and colouring. Either raw or cooked it has a good flavour, and its juiciness helps the flesh dissolve to a light, delicate purée when baked or stewed.

The *Pomona* credited the raising of this apple to *Mr* Peasgood, but the generally agreed story is that his wife Emma started the tree from a pip while still a girl in Grantham, Lincolnshire, in the 1850s. On her marriage to John Peasgood she took the young tree with her to Stamford and its fruit received a First Class Certificate from the RHS in 1872. The great fruitman Thomas Laxton then introduced it to the wider world and it has retained its reputation as a good garden tree ever since.

INTRODUCED	Lincolnshire, 1850s
USES	cooking/eating
HARVEST	mid-September
KEEPING	until December
FLOWERING TIME	0
FERTILITY	partially self-fertile
VIGOUR	quite vigorous, spreading
FRUIT BEARING	spur bearing
DISEASE RESISTANCE	reasonably resistant to mildew and scab; susceptible to canker

Pitmaston Pine Apple

The little Pitmaston Pine Apple is regarded as an apple for the connoisseur. Although it can disappoint after a poor summer, in good years – and especially after a period in storage has intensified the flavours – its distinctive sweet tartness is a delight, with hints of honey and vanilla brightened by a pleasing pineapple-like acidity inherited from its parent, Golden Pippin (*see* Lucombe's Pine, *page 88*).

The tree is small and slender, and puts on a great show of blossom, but its crop is inclined to be erratic and easily falls into a biennial pattern. Thinning the fruitlets quite ruthlessly will help combat this, though probably not overcome it entirely, and also help them grow to their optimum size. Even then, don't expect more than a golfball-sized delicacy.

Pitmaston occurs in a number of fruit names, and not just apples, the introduction of which can be mostly traced back to one man: John Williams (1773–1853) of Pitmaston House on the south-western outskirts of Worcester. The Pitmaston Pine Apple was originally raised, at the end of the eighteenth century, on the estate of Lord Foley at Witley Court, some fifteen miles north, but by 1820 was being grown in Williams's ornamental orchard. His enquiring mind led him to wide-ranging and successful experimentation with hybridization and improved growing conditions; a plaque on Pitmaston House commemorates him as a 'pioneering scientific horticulturalist, plant breeder and meteorologist'.

INTRODUCED	Worcestershire, 1785
USES	eating
HARVEST	early October
KEEPING	until December–January
FLOWERING TIME	0
FERTILITY	self-sterile
VIGOUR	moderate
FRUIT BEARING	spur-bearing; biennial tendency
DISEASE RESISTANCE	good; scab-resistant

Pomeroy

Pomeroy – from *Pomme du Roi* – is a very old name and it is entirely possible that the first Pomeroys (apples and people, for it is a surname too) came over with William the Conqueror. At the time of the *Pomona*, Pomeroys were well known and sought after for their flavour, but such an ancient lineage of course means that pomological genealogy had by then had time to become very blurred and uncertain indeed. Several regions laid claim to their own particular Pomeroy, whether or not it was any different from their neighbours', and they were also classified by season. So the Victorians had on offer the Early, the New and the Old but also the Herefordshire, the Somerset, the Lancashire and other locale-specific variants. The *Pomona* captions the rosier apple on the page 'Pomeroy, aka Herefordshire Pomeroy' but in appearance it is very like the only Pomeroy usually obtainable today… the Somerset. (The other is identified as Winter Pomeroy, more common in Herefordshire at the time, though it was, harrumphed the *Pomona*, frequently marketed 'under the absurd name of "Green Blenheim"', cashing in on the popularity of Blenheim Orange.)

However it is labelled, the 'modern' Pomeroy is a good, flavoursome apple, juicy and with a good crunch followed by a sweet, rich taste (and another with pineapple undertones).

Pomeroy (above) & Winter Pomeroy (below)

INTRODUCED	unknown
USES	eating
HARVEST	mid-October
KEEPING	until January
FLOWERING TIME	0
FERTILITY	self-sterile
VIGOUR	moderate
FRUIT BEARING	spur-bearing
DISEASE RESISTANCE	good

Potts' Seedling

H. Rider Haggard, he of *King Solomon's Mines* and *She*, also had an influential but less known career examining and writing on the contemporary state of agriculture and land use. In volume 2 of his *Rural England* (1906) he reported that during his travels through Cambridgeshire he was told 'Bismarck, Worcester Pearmain, Cox's Orange Pippin and Pott's [*sic*] Seedling … to be the most satisfactory apples'.

Samuel Potts bred his apple in Ashton-under-Lyne, just east of Manchester, in about 1849, reportedly from the pips of an unrecorded American variety. In the *Pomona*, Robert Hogg wrote that he was describing and depicting Potts' Seedling for the first time, and likened it to Lord Suffield (*see page 132*) – the two are illustrated on the same page – praising its cooking qualities but warning about its ease of bruising.

Today, Potts' Seedling is best known as a (probable) parent of James Grieve and probably the least remembered of the varieties commended to Rider Haggard, but throughout the second half of the nineteenth century it was a popular mid-season cooking apple, and can still be appreciated for the smooth purée it produces, sweet enough not to need much, if any, sugar added. It is also particularly decorative when in blossom.

INTRODUCED	Lancashire, 1849
USES	cooking
HARVEST	early September
KEEPING	about a month
FLOWERING TIME	0
FERTILITY	self-sterile
VIGOUR	moderate, spreading
FRUIT BEARING	spur-bearing
DISEASE RESISTANCE	average

Queen

'Large and broader than high, with a shallow crown' does not paint a very complimentary picture of a ruling monarch, but it sums up Queen the apple. Its size and sharp, juice-laden flesh make it a good culinary apple, favoured for baking and pies and also for sauces, as it melts down to a fine bright golden purée. Its natural tartness will probably need to be softened in most recipes with some honey or sugar.

Queen was a very new apple on the market when it was included in the *Pomona*. It had been exhibited for the first time in 1880 (when it received a First Class Certificate from the RHS), by the Chelmsford nursery of Saltmarsh & Son, which had acquired young stock from a farmer in nearby Billericay. It was originally called the Claimant and was also often known as Saltmarsh's Queen.

For many years Queen was a popular fruit tree for the garden, being a good, dependable cropper and an adaptable kitchen apple, even if it didn't keep for very long. The pale blossom gives a lovely springtime show, and the bright, red-streaked apples put on a fine display at the end of the summer. It bruises easily, though, so don't expect a rewarding collection of windfalls.

Queen (left)

INTRODUCED	Essex, mid-nineteenth century
USES	cooking
HARVEST	mid-September
KEEPING	until December, with care
FLOWERING TIME	0/–1
FERTILITY	self-sterile
VIGOUR	moderate
FRUIT BEARING	partially tip-bearing, but freely produces spurs
DISEASE RESISTANCE	good

Red Astrachan

The prime quality of Red Astrachan is Hardiness, with a capital H. As the name suggests, its probable origin was southern Russia – Astrachan straddles the Volga just before it enters the Caspian Sea. The Volga delta hardly claims to have Russia's most extreme climate, but when Red Astrachan arrived in Britain via Sweden in the early nineteenth century it came with a reputation that it could brave the worst weather intact. And so it can. It was one of the apples the Horticultural Society of London (precursor of the RHS) chose to ship to its counterpart in Massachusetts to test 'hardy Russian' varieties in the harsher New England climate. It flourished, spread and by the turn of the twentieth century was one of the most popular varieties from Maine to Miami. It is much less well known in Britain today, but remains easier to find in the USA.

Hardiness and history apart, Red Astrachan's merits are variable. Caught at just the right moment, it makes good eating raw or cooked – and if the flesh is red-stained, the sweet/tart purée has a pretty pink flush. But the brilliant vermilion skin is very thin, making the apples vulnerable to spoiling, even cracking on the tree. The fruit don't keep long either, and are inclined to be biennial, so that sweet moment of perfection may prove elusive.

INTRODUCED	Astrachan, *c*. 1780
USES	cooking/eating
HARVEST	early August
KEEPING	no
FLOWERING TIME	−2
FERTILITY	self-sterile
VIGOUR	vigorous
FRUIT BEARING	spur-bearing; biennial tendency
DISEASE RESISTANCE	susceptible to scab

Reinette du Canada

A misleading name, as this is not a Canadian apple at all, but almost certainly from France; it is still much esteemed there, where it is generally known simply as 'Canada'. However, it was in Britain by 1771 and by early the following century was being planted in North America.

In common with many other reinettes, the Canada is a quality apple, full of flavour. It is also usefully versatile. When first harvested it is very sharp, which recommends it for cooking, especially for tarts and pies as it keeps its shape. After time in storage, though, its taste mellows, the flesh dries to a firm nuttiness and it evolves into a fruit that can be enjoyed raw as well as cooked, and will keep right through to spring.

This apple's only real disadvantage is its looks: not the ugliest kid in the orchard, maybe, but a bit lopsided and knobbly-kneed, with uneven russet mottling giving it an unkempt air. Canada trees give a good show of blossom and grow naturally quite big, although they will tend to develop larger fruit if the tree is restrained by training (*see page 225*).

INTRODUCED	from France, *c.* 1771
USES	cooking/eating
HARVEST	mid-October
KEEPING	until March
FLOWERING TIME	0
FERTILITY	self-sterile – triploid
VIGOUR	vigorous
FRUIT BEARING	spur-bearing
DISEASE RESISTANCE	scab-resistant; susceptible to canker

Ribston Pippin

You get a lot of bang for your buck with a Ribston Pippin: history, looks, versatility and flavour.

This is the apple that was, by general agreement, mother to the two great apples Richard Cox launched on the world: his Pomona and, most famously, his Orange Pippin (*see pages 58 & 56*); directly and through Cox's Orange Pippin its genes have contributed to many excellent apples.

The pip from which the original Ribston Pippin grew was purportedly brought to Ribston Hall in North Yorkshire from Normandy in 1707. The fame of its attractive, richly flavoured, sweet yet tart fruit soon spread and it remains a firm favourite with apple lovers to this day, albeit much less widely grown commercially. It keeps well – indeed its flavour gets even better after a short while in storage – and its underlying acidity makes Ribston a choice apple for pies and cider.

Does this paragon have any disadvantages? Well, it certainly needs watching. Although traditionally said to be ready in late September, the apples don't stay long on the tree: as soon as they are ripe, they drop, so they can catch you on the hop if you don't want to be harvesting only windfalls. The tree is also inclined to send out a lot of whippy new growth that needs pruning back, but it is happy to be trained as an espalier or cordon, which makes the growth more controllable.

INTRODUCED	Yorkshire, *c.* 1707
USES	eating/cooking/cider-making
HARVEST	late September (but see left)
KEEPING	until January
FLOWERING TIME	−1
FERTILITY	self-sterile – triploid
VIGOUR	moderate
FRUIT BEARING	spur-bearing
DISEASE RESISTANCE	resistant to scab; susceptible to canker and mildew

Roxbury Russet

When seeds and saplings accompanied settlers over the Atlantic and westwards across America, they developed and adapted to local conditions, just like the people who planted them – new apples for a new world.

The North American apples that appeared in British markets in the second half of the nineteenth century seduced with their glamour: their size, their smooth shininess, the brilliant scarlet of their skins. As demand grew, much experimentation was done with transplanting young trees back in Britain, but they had changed too completely to thrive in the soil and conditions their ancestors had left maybe 200 years earlier. One of the few to make the repatriation successfully was Roxbury Russet, which is neither shiny nor scarlet.

Roxbury Russet's forebears must have crossed from Europe very early; by the early 1600s it had established itself as a recognized New England apple, named after the Massachusetts town in which it originated (it's also often called Boston Russet). Reared to cope with harsh winters, it is extremely hardy, and the apples keep well. Like most russets, the flesh is firm and a little chewy rather than running with juice, but it is pleasingly sweet and aromatic yet tangy; there's even a hint of cider, especially once it's been stored for a while.

INTRODUCED	Massachusetts, early seventeenth century
USES	eating/cider-making
HARVEST	mid-October
KEEPING	until March, sometimes beyond
FLOWERING TIME	0
FERTILITY	self-sterile triploid
VIGOUR	moderate
FRUIT BEARING	spur-bearing
DISEASE RESISTANCE	good resistance to mildew and scab

Scarlet Nonpareil

Nonpareil – an apple without equal? Perhaps not quite, given all the other 'Nonpareils', 'Nonsuches' and 'Incomparables' that jostle for apple stardom, but an apple worth seeking out all the same. The original Nonpareil is believed to have arrived from France in the middle of the sixteenth century and became more highly esteemed in England than in its native land. It is probable that the Scarlet Nonpareil, which is very similar and equally tasty but with more brilliant colouring, has the 'old' Nonpareil as one of its parents. It was spotted in the garden of a pub in Esher, Surrey, in the 1770s, its qualities recognized, and was soon on offer to an appreciative market. It was given an Award of Merit in 1901.

Scarlet Nonpareil's flavour is, after a good summer, a really lovely balance of the sweet and the sharp. It can be harvested in October, but will benefit from being left unpicked for as long as the weather permits (unlike some varieties, it lasts well on the tree), so that its flavour can intensify. Given its southern origins and its need for sun, this is probably an apple for the warmer counties. The tree is not a large one, but is graceful and slender – the original Nonpareil was popularly grown in pots in formal gardens to show off its beautiful pink blossom and neat fruit, and the Scarlet is similarly ornamental.

INTRODUCED	Surrey, *c.* 1773
USES	eating
HARVEST	mid-October
KEEPING	until March
FLOWERING TIME	0
FERTILITY	self-sterile
VIGOUR	moderate
FRUIT BEARING	spur-bearing
DISEASE RESISTANCE	good

Schoolmaster

Schoolmaster was a new apple on the scene when the *Pomona* was published, but the compilers were enthusiastic – 'a very excellent culinary apple' – and, understandably, were keen to claim it for Herefordshire. An alternative claim, which seems more likely, is that the tree was found in the grounds of Old Stamford Grammar School. It was introduced in 1880 by the renowned nurseryman Thomas Laxton; until he moved to Bedford in 1879, Laxton's home and business had been in Stamford. Three years later the report of the National Apple Congress described the samples Laxton had submitted as being 'large and extremely fine – a very promising apple'.

It became a favourite for commercial growers for canning, but Schoolmaster never quite made it to the top of the class. However, it's a good cooking apple, with pleasing looks and proportions, and it produces heavy crops each year. The flesh is very acidic and froths up beautifully for puddings and sauces. It has the added advantage of not discolouring, which makes it a good raw addition to, for example, a shredded salad.

INTRODUCED	*c.* 1855
USES	cooking
HARVEST	mid-October
KEEPING	until January
FLOWERING TIME	0
FERTILITY	self-sterile
VIGOUR	moderate
FRUIT BEARING	spur-bearing
DISEASE RESISTANCE	average

Stirling Castle

Unsurprisingly, this large cooking apple is popular in Scotland, but should be more widely grown elsewhere. It makes a small, spreading tree that crops well. The sharp, acid flesh cooks down to an excellent-flavoured purée. One of Stirling Castle's additional assets is its frost-resistance. While it is not particularly late into bloom, its petals have a greater substance than many; this and the protective, cupped shape of its individual flowers allow it to stand up to cold snaps that might be the downfall of frailer blossoms.

Stirling Castle was introduced to the market by the Stirling-based firm of Drummond's in 1831. However, it was known in the area before then, and John Christie is generally credited with raising it in his nursery at Causewayhead, just across the Forth from Stirling. The National Apple Congress in 1883 brought it to the attention of growers nationwide, when it was acclaimed by apple enthusiasts north and south of the border.

Its keeping qualities vary according to location. In the south it is best used soon after picking, and certainly within the month, whereas in the north and in its native Scotland it seems to keep much more satisfactorily, even up to Christmas.

INTRODUCED	Scotland, 1820s (first recorded 1831)
USES	cooking
HARVEST	mid-September
KEEPING	until December
FLOWERING TIME	0
FERTILITY	reasonably self-fertile
VIGOUR	small
FRUIT BEARING	spur-bearing, heavy cropper
DISEASE RESISTANCE	slightly susceptible to mildew; very scab-resistant

Striped Beefing

Beaufin, Biffin, Beefin, Beefing… that's the usual assumption of the evolution of the Beefing family name, but the *Pomona* prefers the plausible explanation that 'Beaufin' emerged as a Frenchified refinement of 'Beefing', referring to 'the similarity that the dried fruit presents to beef'.

Like the Herefordshire and Norfolk Beefings (*see pages 102 & 152*), the Striped is esteemed as a culinary apple. It is larger than both its cousins and if possible even more good-looking, more *beau fin*. The influential fruit expert George Lindley noticed a tree bearing these striking fruit in a garden in Lakenham (now swallowed up into the suburbs of Norwich), and on measuring one of the apples recorded its circumference as 12½ inches (32 cm).

Mr Lindley made his discovery in 1794, but it was another fifty years before Striped Beefing found its way on to the market, after the great pomologist Robert Hogg had been given graft material to propagate. Dr Hogg called it 'noble … one of the best culinary apples in cultivation'. Its puréed flesh is especially moreish, and because it softens and intensifies rather than fluffs it makes a first-rate baking apple. By the new year it makes a good, if rather large, eater, and will last in a cool store until Easter or even, allegedly, until the apple trees are blossoming again.

INTRODUCED	Norfolk, 1794
USES	cooking/eating
HARVEST	early October
KEEPING	until April
FLOWERING TIME	−1
FERTILITY	self-sterile – triploid
VIGOUR	moderate, spreading
FRUIT BEARING	spur-bearing
DISEASE RESISTANCE	good

Sturmer Pippin

A vital fact to know about Sturmer Pippins is that they are *not* apples to be enjoyed straight off the tree. Although technically they may be ripe in October or November, it is best to leave them unpicked as long as the weather will allow and then carefully store them at least until after Christmas, and until February or March if possible. The reward for this patience is the small miracle of unpalatably harsh-tasting flesh having turned into a sweet, richly aromatic and flavourful treat.

Sturmer Pippin is named after the small village on the Essex–Suffolk border where it was first raised by the memorably named Ezekiel Dillstone. His cross between Nonpareil and Ribston Pippin (*see page 170*) was a big hit in nineteenth-century dining rooms, where sweet fresh fruit was scarce between Christmas and the new season's cherries.

Sturmers really need a good, warm summer to store up sufficient sugar potential for their transformation. When Thomas Dillstone took some of his grandfather's Sturmer scion wood to Tasmania he found the trees thrived. They were part of the foundation of the Australian apple industry; records for 1934 show 800,000 bushels of Sturmers being exported back to the UK – that's some 100 million apples.

INTRODUCED	Essex, 1831
USES	eating
HARVEST	late October
KEEPING	until at least March, possibly to May
FLOWERING TIME	0
FERTILITY	partially self-fertile
VIGOUR	moderate
FRUIT BEARING	spur-bearing
DISEASE RESISTANCE	susceptible to canker

Summer Golden Pippin

'One of the most delicious summer apples,' enthused the *Pomona*, 'and ought to form one of every collection, however small.' Small is the key word here – this is one of the apple world's daintier trees; indeed, in the nineteenth century Summer Golden Pippin was a popular variety for growing in pots. Even though the *Pomona* boasts that it is inclined to grow larger in Herefordshire than elsewhere, this is never going to make a very large tree, even on a non-dwarfing rootstock. Don't confuse it with the much larger Golden Pippin (*see page 88*).

The fruit, too, are small – golden orbs just 5 cm (2 in.) across. They are highly decorative, hanging from the tree like small lit lanterns, and they have a fine rich flavour (they won't keep, so enjoy them fresh from the tree).

Summer Golden Pippin is the parent of several other heritage apples, including Yellow Ingestrie (*see page 198*), which is also sometimes marketed as Summer Golden Pippin.

INTRODUCED	England, by 1800
USES	eating
HARVEST	late August
KEEPING	a month or less
FLOWERING TIME	–1
FERTILITY	self-sterile
VIGOUR	moderate
FRUIT BEARING	spur-bearing
DISEASE RESISTANCE	good

Tom Putt

Was Tom Putt named after a churchman in Somerset? Or a landowner in Devon? Is the apple a Dorset native or, as the *Pomona* asserts, a Herefordshire variety, called Tom Potter in Devon? But, *pace* the *Pomona*, the rosy cider apple we know today appears to be the West Country variety. The two Thomas Putts continue to confuse, but as the Rev. Tom Putt of Trent (Somerset/Dorset border) was the nephew of Thomas Putt of Combe House, Gittisham (Devon), and as the reverend moved to Combe House after his uncle's death, and 250 years of history can mist the facts, we should perhaps award them equal honours.

Whatever the truth behind the name, Tom Putt is a valuable variety, growing into a low, spreading tree that withstands adverse conditions, particularly windy, exposed sites. The apples it produces are good-looking, richly striped scarlet and usually more distinctly ribbed than Alice Ellis's painting shows. Its primary role is as a cider apple, producing an admirable sharp, dry juice. However, it is quite large and good for cooking, too, when it sweetens considerably. Once harvested, the fruit keeps for at least a couple of months, although the skin toughens in storage.

INTRODUCED	Dorset, 1700s
USES	cider-making/cooking
HARVEST	late August–early September
KEEPING	until November or December
FLOWERING TIME	0
FERTILITY	self-sterile – triploid
VIGOUR	vigorous, spreading
FRUIT BEARING	spur-bearing
DISEASE RESISTANCE	very scab-resistant; prone to canker and apple sawfly

Tower of Glamis

There seems to be no evidence that this traditional old Scottish favourite was first bred at the castle, but the name serves the apple well. It conjures up images of the romantic, turreted castle that has been the focus of centuries of royal history, from the bloody times of Macbeth ('Thane of Glamis ... that shalt be king hereafter') and Robert the Bruce to the gentler era of Queen Elizabeth The Queen Mother's childhood.

By 1800 Tower of Glamis was widely grown in orchards throughout Clydesdale and the fruit-growing district of Carse of Gowrie, proving itself a good choice for colder climes and well suited to exposed conditions.

The large, light-green fruits have a crisp, perfumed flesh that has attracted descriptions varying from 'bland' to 'well-flavoured' – yet another example of how *terroir* and conditions can influence taste. And can you taste Tower of Glamis at Glamis Castle? Most certainly. The head gardener reports that their young trees, including two espaliers in the walled garden, are proving themselves healthy and disease-resistant. They are now producing fruit served in the visitors' restaurant, and the kitchens say 'it stews down very well, not too wet, not too dry and good flavour'.

INTRODUCED	Scotland, by 1800
USES	cooking
HARVEST	early October
KEEPING	until December
FLOWERING TIME	−1
FERTILITY	self-sterile – triploid
VIGOUR	vigorous
FRUIT BEARING	spur-bearing
DISEASE RESISTANCE	generally good; slightly susceptible to scab

Warner's King

Two hundred years ago this was an immensely popular culinary apple, widely planted in all the main apple-growing areas. It suffered, along with many other cookers, from the rise and rise of the Bramley (*see page 40*), but is well worth seeking out. It rewards with a heavy crop, and the very large, pale green-gold fruit – not always as flushed as in this painting – cook down into a strong-flavoured purée with a good tart bite. The blossom adds to its charms, the flowers opening from deep pink buds, and the variety is robust enough to make it a good recommendation for colder, windy regions.

Mr Warner was an eighteenth-century Kentish appleman, but the tree that bears his name appears to have acquired a slew of other names, depending on where it was planted and who was growing it. Many Victorians knew it as the King Apple or Killick's Apple (confusingly, Lewis Killick put his name to more than one variety – *see* Loddington, *page 124*). The *Pomona* contains a lengthy account of how Mr Killick sought out and identified many Warner's King trees masquerading under other names in his own orchard, including 'Nelson's Glory and D T Fish (might this be how one record of the apple's name in Russia is 'Fish'?).

INTRODUCED	Kent, *c.* 1700
USES	cooking/cider-making
HARVEST	late September
KEEPING	until December
FLOWERING TIME	−1
FERTILITY	self-sterile – triploid
VIGOUR	vigorous
FRUIT BEARING	spur-bearing
DISEASE RESISTANCE	susceptible to scab, canker and bitter pit

Wheeler's Russet

If you're looking for a beautiful blossom tree bearing good crops of rich-tasting apples that will serve for both eating and cooking, but is hardy enough to stand up to a cold, wet climate, then this could be the one for you. Wheeler's Russet was raised in Gloucestershire (though which Mr Wheeler it was named after is in doubt), and for much of its history has been known to thrive in Scotland and the Welsh mountains. This is a variety that has been around for at least 300 years: it appears in *The Practical Husbandman and Planter*, a 1733 publication; and Philip Miller, head gardener at Chelsea Physic Garden for nearly fifty years (1722–70), included it in his shortlist of 'the sort of apples proper for Espaliers'.

When freshly picked the apples are juicy but tart, and better used for cooking; however, they store well in their all-over russet jackets and by the new year have developed a sweetness that make them a pleasing eating apple over the winter. Recent cell analysis has shown that Wheeler's Russet may be a triploid variety; this was inconclusive, but it may be wise to treat it as such to ensure its pollination needs are met (*see page 222*).

Wheeler's Russet is also sometimes given as a synonym for Acklam Russet, but this is a later-bred Yorkshire variety, smaller and more highly coloured, which ripens slightly earlier.

INTRODUCED	Gloucestershire, *c.* 1717
USES	cooking/eating
HARVEST	late October
KEEPING	until March
FLOWERING TIME	0
FERTILITY	self-sterile – possibly triploid
VIGOUR	moderate
FRUIT BEARING	spur-bearing
DISEASE RESISTANCE	scab-resistant

Worcester Pearmain

Along with Cox and Bramley, this is probably one of the more familiar varieties in this book. In the nineteenth century Worcester was at the core, if you'll forgive the pun, of England's fruit-growing enterprises, and it was near the city that Thomas Smith established St John's Nurseries. The business expanded under his son and grandson (both Richards), and before the end of the nineteenth century it claimed to be one of the largest plant nurseries in the world.

We can thank grandson Richard for Worcester Pearmain. For £10 he acquired from a neighbour the exclusive rights to grafting material of a promising rosy red apple. In 1875 it was awarded a First Class Certificate, and it became the leading commercially planted apple. It is the parent of many popular varieties, including Discovery, Katy, Lord Lambourne and Tydeman's Early Worcester.

This is an apple that doesn't always reach its potential. It is always good, but only sometimes great; in a kind year, however, its sweet juiciness and crisp flesh are enhanced by an aromatic 'strawberriness' inherited from its parent, Devonshire Quarrenden (*see page 62*). The apples benefit from being left on the tree for as long as the weather allows.

Worcester Pearmain's beautiful blossom doesn't easily succumb to frost, contributing to its reliability as a cropper. Although the cold doesn't worry it, damp does, which makes it vulnerable to scab and especially canker.

INTRODUCED	Worcester, 1870s
USES	eating
HARVEST	early September
KEEPING	until October
FLOWERING TIME	o
FERTILITY	partially self-fertile
VIGOUR	moderate
FRUIT BEARING	tip-bearing
DISEASE RESISTANCE	susceptible to canker, scab; very resistant to mildew

Wyken Pippin

For Victorians this was a top-ten dessert apple, appreciated for its fruity aroma and rich taste. The Wyken (pronounced *Why*–) was known from early in the eighteenth century as an apple grown on the land of Lord Craven at Wyken, near Coventry, possibly from a pip brought back from the Netherlands by Admiral Thomas Craven.

Although only small, this golden freckled apple has a great, punchy flavour, and firm, juicy flesh. These qualities (plus, perhaps, the fact that it produces a generous number of pips) led the Laxton brothers to use it in their apple breeding at the turn of the twentieth century: both Laxton's Superb and Laxton's Pearmain are Wyken Pippin crossed with Cox's Orange Pippin.

Although a moderately vigorous grower, Wyken makes a slender, upright tree that doesn't produce many side branches – and, because it is primarily a tip-bearer, this means that, left to its own devices, it would only produce a few fruit each year. Therefore careful formative pruning is needed to encourage it to bush out and produce more than its natural meagre count of branches, and so have more branch tips on which blossom and fruit can form (*see page 233*).

INTRODUCED	Coventry, early eighteenth century
USES	eating
HARVEST	mid-October
KEEPING	until January
FLOWERING TIME	0
FERTILITY	self-sterile
VIGOUR	moderate
FRUIT BEARING	tip-bearing
DISEASE RESISTANCE	scab-resistant; susceptible to bitter pit

Yellow & Red Ingestrie

Twins! The Yellow and Red Ingestrie were not just bred from pips and pollen of the same varieties (Orange Pippin x Golden Pippin) but the pips came from the same individual Orange Pippin apple. But they are fraternal, not identical, twins, and a good example of just how unpredictable apple breeding can be.

The Red Ingestrie, though well known throughout the nineteenth century, had faded to oblivion by the end of the First World War; it has only recently been rediscovered (*see* Bernwode Fruit Trees, *page 243*). The Yellow Ingestrie, the smaller, unflushed twin, is much more widely available; its graceful, semi-weeping habit makes it an admirable garden tree, beautiful in blossom and especially when laden with its pretty little golden fruit. The soft colouring suggests the apples themselves may be soft and flaccid, but when the tree is thriving the intensity of their flavour is a wonderful surprise.

The breeder responsible for these little apples was Thomas Andrew Knight, the first of the great apple hybridizers, and he named them after the grand Jacobean Ingestre Hall in Staffordshire, home of his friend Lord Talbot – but to Victorian shoppers in London markets they were known simply as 'Summers'.

Red Ingestrie (left) and Yellow Ingestrie (right)

INTRODUCED	Herefordshire, *c.* 1800
USES	eating
HARVEST	early September
KEEPING	about a month
FLOWERING TIME	0/−1
FERTILITY	semi-sterile
VIGOUR	small, semi-weeping
FRUIT BEARING	spur-bearing
DISEASE RESISTANCE	generally good, though the Red can attract scab

Yorkshire Greening

This is one of several apples that has attracted the alternative name of Seek No Further, but one of Yorkshire Greening's more appropriately descriptive synonyms is Yorkshire Goose Sauce. The fruity but very sharp purée it produces is the perfect accompaniment to a fatty meat such as goose or pork. It is one of the many good cookers that long ago lost ground to the ubiquitous Bramley, but it is highly prized, among those who know it, for apple puddings and crumbles.

As a Yorkshire apple – claimed by Pontefract and York among other locations – it is a good variety for colder regions; the trees are very hardy and have a wide rather than tall habit of growth, equipping them well for a windy site, and they can be relied on to crop profusely.

Yorkshire Greening had a reputation for keeping exceptionally long in storage, nine or ten months according to some accounts, but this may be expecting a little too much of it. But stored well it should keep until the spring, sweetening with age, as all apples do, but not enough to be considered an enticing eater. However, its acidity makes it a useful addition for sharpening cider.

INTRODUCED	Yorkshire, *c.* 1803
USES	cooking
HARVEST	mid-October
KEEPING	until March
FLOWERING TIME	0/−1
FERTILITY	self-sterile – triploid
VIGOUR	small but spreading
FRUIT BEARING	spur-bearing
DISEASE RESISTANCE	good

Claygate Pearmain

The Claygate Pearmain was listed among the 'new and remarkable Varieties of Fruits, ripened in the Summer and Autumn of the Year 1822, which were exhibited at Meetings of the Horticultural Society'. John Braddick, a Surrey fruit-grower, had spotted an apple sapling in a hedgerow, grown it on and named it after the village of its origin: Claygate, near Esher. Following its favourable reception at the Horticultural Society of London it became a popular and appreciated variety throughout the nineteenth century. The RHS gave it an Award of Merit in 1901 and a First Class Certificate in 1921; today it holds the coveted AGM.

NOTABLE ABSENTEES
While wide-ranging and painstakingly compiled, *The Herefordshire Pomona* was not, could not have been, completely comprehensive. These last few apples are among those that did not find a place in the *Pomona* but were acclaimed at the time and remain of great interest today.

It's a good-looking apple, typically slightly larger than a Cox's Orange Pippin (*see page 56*), and takes on a rich red flush to its skin on the side exposed to the sun. It's a wonderfully complex taste-teaser, especially after a good summer. Despite being slightly soft rather than crisp, the flesh is refreshingly juicy, and some have also detected pineapple undertones to the flavour. Some russeting, which is very variable, provides a slight nuttiness, and the great flavour deepens even further after a little keeping.

Triploid varieties are often notably large and rangy, but Claygate Pearmain is surprisingly neat and moderately sized, but has a triploid's typical resistance to disease and is a good choice for a wide range of growing conditions, especially in colder, wetter districts. It is also a reliable cropper.

INTRODUCED	Surrey, *c.* 1821
USES	eating
HARVEST	early October
KEEPING	about two months
FLOWERING TIME	0
FERTILITY	self-sterile – triploid
VIGOUR	moderate, upright
FRUIT BEARING	partially tip-bearing but produces plenty of spurs
DISEASE RESISTANCE	resistant to scab and mildew

Egremont Russet

Russets have always had a following, though their popularity is periodically eclipsed by smooth, shiny-skinned apples. The Egremont is not just tentatively russeted; its skin is typically completely covered in a fine suede overcoat. It is also perhaps the best-known russet today, and one of the few grown in serious commercial quantities.

Picked too early the fruit can be plain cardboardy – how many have been put off by under-ripe supermarket Egremonts? One helpful indicator is to wait until the skin has developed a slight red blush to its dull greeny-gold. Then its delicious, harmonious sweet-sharpness, overlaid by the nutty russet, comes into its own. A great favourite to serve with cheese, and enthusiasts say that, despite its lack of juiciness, it also makes an interesting and excellent cider.

The tree is a heavy cropper (though old trees can become biennial); it thrives even in exposed regions and is resistant to most apple diseases except bitter pit. Egremont Russet was introduced to the world by J. Scott of Somerset just as the *Pomona* was being conceived, but its origins are uncertain. Records at Petworth House (Sussex), the ancestral home of the Earls of Egremont, cannot confirm the popular theory that it was raised there, although the extensive family estates do also include land at the other end of England, around Egremont Castle, Cumbria.

INTRODUCED	1872
USES	eating
HARVEST	late September
KEEPING	until January
FLOWERING TIME	−1
FERTILITY	self-sterile
VIGOUR	moderate
FRUIT BEARING	spur-bearing
DISEASE RESISTANCE	resistant to scab, mildew and canker; prone to bitter pit

Orleans Reinette

Orleans Reinette was on the scene long before the *Pomona*, but rose to prominence in Britain only when Edward Bunyard enthused about it in the early twentieth century. Bunyard (1878–1939) knew his apples – he came from a family of Kentish growers and was famed as a gastronome – and his opinions were highly influential. Orleans Reinette was, in his view, 'the best apple grown in Western Europe'. He particularly recommended it to be kept for Christmas to enjoy with a glass of port.

And here comes the problem. Growers, both amateur and professional, have very different experiences of Orleans Reinette, especially its keeping properties. For some it matures beautifully by December, with lovely festive hints of citrus and nutmeg; for others it barely lasts two or three weeks in store. Part of this variability may lie in the picking, not so much when but how. Orleans has an extremely short, stubby stalk. If the apples are not very carefully turned to release them from the branch they can leave the stalk behind, allowing an opening for rot in the top of the fruit. It is never a heavy bearer and flourishes best in warmth; cool and damp increase its susceptibility to diseases such as scab.

To see what an Orleans Reinette looks like, see page 39, as it resembles the Blenheim Orange in size and colouring. However, it varies a great deal; its russeting, for example, may be just a light dusting of pale tan freckles or a full rusty armour.

INTRODUCED	pre-1776
USES	eating/cooking/cider
HARVEST	mid-October
KEEPING	a month or two, with care
FLOWERING TIME	+1
FERTILITY	self-sterile – triploid
VIGOUR	moderate
FRUIT BEARING	spur-bearing; biennial tendency
DISEASE RESISTANCE	generally good and mildew-resistant *(but see left)*

Rosemary Russet

The heart-shaped Rosemary Russet is often compared to Ashmead's Kernel in the intensity and moreishness of its flavour – high praise indeed (*see page 28*). Its appeal at first sight is perhaps more immediate than the better known Ashmead's, as it has a brighter colouring, with streaks of orange-red partly overlaid by a crazed mottling of patchy russet. A quality apple.

It was raised by the renowned Ronalds Nursery in Brentford, Middlesex, and Hugh Ronalds featured it in his *Pyrus Malus Brentfordiensis* (1831), where he called it simply the Rosemary Apple. He describes it as 'a little red and russety on the outside; the fruit is firm and of a high rich flavour. A very hardy, productive, useful sort, either for the table or kitchen use.' So, although nowadays it is usually designated an eating apple, there is good reason for its sweet-sharp acidity to recommend it for cooking.

Rosemary Russet is usually found to be a good cropper, though not necessarily prolific. One of its additional assets is its particularly beautiful flowers, of an unusual pink (at least among apple blossoms) that tends towards the peachy rather than the plummy.

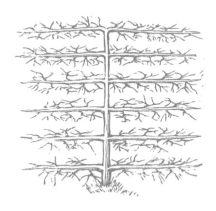

INTRODUCED	Middlesex, early nineteenth century
USES	eating
HARVEST	October
KEEPING	until the end of the year, with care until March
FLOWERING TIME	0
FERTILITY	self-sterile
VIGOUR	vigorous, upright
FRUIT BEARING	spur-bearing
DISEASE RESISTANCE	good; resistant to mildew, canker and scab

Saint Edmund's Pippin

This often overlooked russet is, for many cognoscenti, superior even to its much more widely grown cousin, Egremont Russet (*see page 204*). Like most apples appreciated for their sophisticated flavour, it does need to be left to ripen fully or it will disappoint, but a Saint Edmund's at its best is a wonderful combination of a honey sweetness counterbalanced by an underlying fruity acidity.

The name suggests its origins: the Suffolk town of Bury St Edmunds, where it was raised by R. Harvey, who named it after the town's saint – often forgotten now, but King Edmund, who was martyred for his faith in 869, was England's patron saint for nearly 500 years before St George took on that mantle. Harvey's apple is quietly attractive, similar in size to a Cox (*see page 56*) but slightly squatter, its old-gold skin overlaid with a silvery sheen of light russeting. The RHS acknowledged its fine qualities with a First Class Certificate in 1875.

The tree is tidy in its habit, not fussy as to conditions, and is a reliable cropper. It is also generally a robustly healthy variety – so one that should be high on the Wanted list for fans of russet apples.

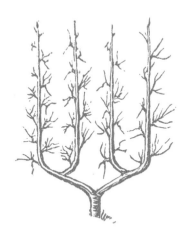

INTRODUCED	Suffolk, mid-nineteenth century
USES	eating/cider-making and juicing
HARVEST	mid September
KEEPING	until October
FLOWERING TIME	−1
FERTILITY	self-sterile
VIGOUR	small
FRUIT BEARING	partially tip-bearing
DISEASE RESISTANCE	highly resistant to scab; some resistance to mildew and canker

Scotch Bridget

Who knows which Scottish lass might have inspired the name, but Scotch Bridget's appearance suggests a cheerful girl, rather plump, her cheeks glowing with laughter. The fresh green, red-flushed fruits are distinctly ribbed, which can give them a slightly lopsided look – easy-going and rustic, rather than smart and urban.

Although this is primarily considered a culinary apple – the flesh softens but doesn't fluff or collapse – the flavour is sufficiently mild that after it has been allowed to concentrate its sugars in storage for a couple of months Scotch Bridget becomes a dual-purpose apple. It is not very strong or distinctive-tasting, and growers in the 'soft south' have found its delicate flavour can border on the flavourless, but this improves markedly in fruit grown in harsher conditions further north, which seem to suit it better.

Scotch Bridget is irrefutably hardy; its willingness to grow and fruit well even after a cool, wet summer made it a popular variety not only in its native Scotland but over the border in the damp orchards of Cumbria and Lancashire, which became its 'second home' right up until the 1950s.

INTRODUCED	Scotland, 1851
USES	cooking/eating
HARVEST	early October
KEEPING	until the end of the year
FLOWERING TIME	0
FERTILITY	self-sterile – triploid
VIGOUR	medium
FRUIT BEARING	spur-bearing
DISEASE RESISTANCE	good

Sops-in-Wine

This last apple is, to be honest, more a curiosity than a 'must-have'. There is a small but growing trend among pomophiles for raising apples with red-stained flesh, bred to reveal a startling strawberry- or plum-coloured interior when cut open. (This is more than a novelty; there is much interest in the health benefits of anthocyanins – the chemical compounds that give fruit and vegetables such as aubergines and raspberries their colour.)

Red-fleshed apples are often presented as a recent development, but 'sops-in-wine' was a descriptive name given to a number of old apples displaying this unusual tendency. The Sops-in-Wine available today is known to date back to the early nineteenth century, possibly earlier.

The highly aromatic fruit are deep crimson, but the degree to which the actual flesh appears wine-soaked will vary from year to year and is highly influenced by the weather. What the apples need is a long growing season to allow them to ripen fully, but also for the night temperatures to drop sufficiently for the anthocyanins to develop and work their magic. So Sops-in-Wine may live up to its name one year, and the following year may offer nothing more than a faint pink tinge. But it does have other attractive attributes: the deep pinkish red extends to its flowers, the new leaves and even the wood, so when well grown this makes a fine ornamental tree. It is also often a heavy cropper, so in most years the immature fruits will need severely thinning in June.

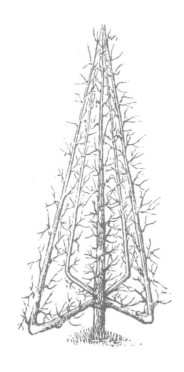

INTRODUCED	described 1832, but probably earlier
USES	eating/cider-making
HARVEST	late August onwards
KEEPING	use fresh
FLOWERING TIME	−2
FERTILITY	self-sterile
VIGOUR	moderately vigorous
FRUIT BEARING	spur-bearing
DISEASE RESISTANCE	susceptible to scab and mildew; fairly canker-resistant

Flowering & pollination times

Apples fall into pollination groups according to when they flower.
The best way to ensure effective pollination, essential to a bountiful crop,
is to plant apples from adjacent flowering groups together (*see p. 221*).
The table below shows relative flowering times of individual apples: the
light green band represents the complete flowering time for each apple,
with the dark green square showing the peak flowering period.

Adam's Pearmain				
Alexander				
Allen's Everlasting				
Annie Elizabeth				
Api				
Ashmead's Kernel				
Beauty of Kent				
Bedfordshire Foundling				
Bess Pool				
Betty Geeson				
Blenheim Orange				
Bramley's Seedling				
Calville Blanc d'Hiver				
Catshead				
Cellini				
Claygate Pearmain				
Cornish Aromatic				
Cornish Gilliflower				
Court of Wick				
Court Pendu Plat				
Cox's Orange Pippin				

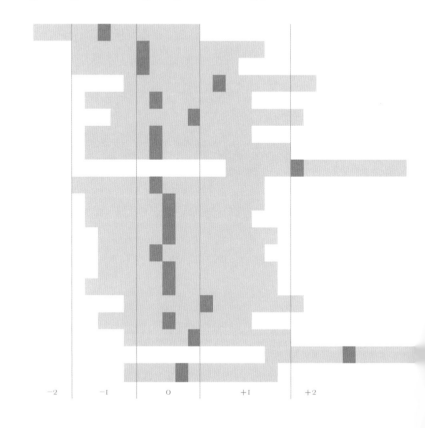

−2   −1   0   +1   +2

Cox's Pomona
D'Arcy Spice
Devonshire Quarrenden
Duchess of Oldenburg
Duchess's Favourite
Duck's Bill
Dumelow's Seedling
Early Julyan
Ecklinville
Egremont Russet
Fearn's Pippin
Forge
Gladstone
Gloria Mundi
Golden Harvey
Golden Noble
Golden Pippin
Golden Spire
Gravenstein
Grenadier
Hanwell Souring
Harvey
Hawthornden
Herefordshire Beefing
Irish Peach
Kentish Fillbasket
Kerry Pippin
Keswick Codlin
King of the Pippins
Kingston Black
Lady Henniker
Lamb Abbey Pearmain
Lane's Prince Albert
Lemon Pippin
Loddington
London Pippin
Lord Burghley
Lord Derby
Lord Suffield

−2   −1   0   +1   +2

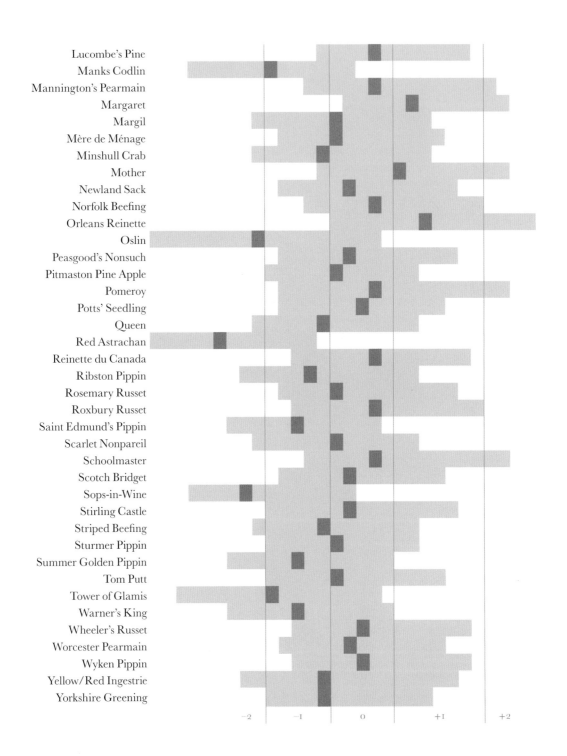

Choosing your trees

There is no single perfect variety of apple. Your choice will depend on your requirements, preferences and the conditions you can offer. So, having decided you would like to grow one or more heritage varieties of your own, here are few initial questions to ask before you buy.

What are my favourite apples?

There is no point in growing a variety that doesn't appeal to you, so this is where the pleasurable research starts – by discovering the possibilities that are out there.

Apples have a surprising range of flavours and textures. Do you prefer sweet or sharp? Crisp and firm or soft and creamy? Juicy or dry? These are qualities that are not possible to convey adequately in words – to understand how an apple can have 'undertones of strawberry' or be pleasing though dry is something you need to experience for yourself. Throughout the season try different apples at farm shops and markets, visit orchards for tasting days, talk to apple-growing neighbours (*see pages 241–3 for some leads*). Draw up a shortlist, both of specific varieties that you like (and don't like) and of general characteristics that you want in an apple.

How will I use my apples?

Do you primarily want the joy of eating apples fresh off the tree, or to use them in cooking? Would you like to store some for the winter? Does crushing for juice (or cider) appeal? If you would like a medley of fruits for different seasons and reasons but don't have room for a full-size orchard, see TRAINING (*page 224*) for ideas on how to accommodate apples in a small space.

A whole orchard or a single tree?

If you have room for eight to ten trees (or more), then you have the luxury of choosing several different varieties, with different ripening times to extend your season, and indulging in a mix of flavours, both for eating and for cooking. But even the smallest garden can accommodate a couple of cordons or 'step-over' apples, which take up hardly any room (*see page 225*).

What conditions am I offering?

Soil can be improved, but the climate is less tractable. Consider whether you need hardy varieties bred to stand up to harsh weather. Similarly, if your garden is much wetter or drier than average, look for varieties suited to those conditions. It is very frustrating to see your crop blown to the ground before it is ripe, so if your proposed site is exposed to high winds, can you provide any sort of windbreak?

Are there other apple trees nearby?

This is important because most varieties are not self-pollinating – they need pollen from a different variety in order to set fruit. This is not an issue in many urban and village gardens, where there will probably be a sufficient range of other apple trees in the vicinity, but if your trees will be more isolated, you will need to provide cross-pollinating varieties yourself – see POLLINATION below.

What else should I consider?

- ⇒ Heritage varieties often have strong links to a particular area. Is this important for you?
- ⇒ Is a bumper harvest a priority, or would you put other qualities ahead of quantity?
- ⇒ Is natural disease resistance important, and are you prepared to apply treatments, should they be needed?

The next few pages aim to guide you towards answers to these questions and help demystify what should be an exciting and rewarding experience: growing your own apples.

Pollination

Most of the apples in this book are described as self-sterile, which means they need to be fertilized by another, different variety. Even self-fertile varieties produce more successfully if they are not reliant on their own pollen.

If there is a mix of apple trees in the neighbourhood, you may not need to give pollination a second thought. Otherwise, you will need to plan for trees that will cross-pollinate each other. To do this, they need to flower at approximately the same time. Apple blossom usually lasts for two or three weeks, but the pollen remains fresh and viable for a much shorter time, typically just three or four days when the flowers are at their peak.

To help distinguish which varieties are suitable for cross-pollination, apples are often categorized in 'pollination groups', typically 1–6 or A–F, with 1 or A being the earliest flowering. However, there is no standardization for these bands, so Supplier Y's Group D, for example, may not be quite the same as Supplier Z's Group 4. The National Fruit Collection's database, collected over many years in the NFC's orchards in Kent, provides dates for 10 per cent flowering, full flowering and 90 per cent petal fall. As they point out, the given dates may hold true *on average* for south-eastern England, but will vary year by year according to the weather conditions, and may slip by up to a month in the north.

However, irrespective of actual dates, relative flowering times for varieties stay reasonably constant in any given location (i.e. exposed to the same weather and growing conditions). With this in mind, the table of FLOWERING & POLLINATION TIMES (*pages 216–18*) shows the flowering period for all the apples in this book *in relation to each other*. This allows you to see at a glance how closely flowering times coincide. Almost half the apples in this book reach peak fertility within a five-day cluster, so for many varieties the choice of pollination partner is very wide. As a more general guide in the individual apple profiles, varieties that fall within the common central cluster are indicated as 0. Varieties that flower earlier are designated as –1 (–2 for exceptionally early); those that flower later are designated as +1 (+2 for exceptionally late), and if you are contemplating one of these varieties, you should pay closer attention to its pollination needs.

A few apples flower so early or so late that few other varieties are in bloom at the same time. An example of this is the very late flowering Court Pendu Plat (*see page 54*). But all is not lost. It is possible to choose a rootstock for it that advances the flowering date slightly (*see* ROOTSTOCKS *below*) or carefully select a cross-pollinator that is almost as late and that wouldn't mind a slightly shadier situation that will further delay its flowering by a day or two. Another tree to throw into the mix is the native crab apple, *Malus sylvestris*, which can be a useful pollinator.

Some apples, including a number in this book, are classified as TRIPLOID, meaning they have three sets of chromosomes. One effect of this is that they are inclined to be poor fertilizers, both of themselves and of other trees. If you choose a triploid variety, you will need *two* other varieties from the same flowering group, which will pollinate each other and also the triploid tree. The only way round this, if space is limited to two trees, is to choose a self-fertile as your second tree. Before you dismiss triploids as being 'awkward', they include some very good varieties that make up for their fertility shortcomings with other qualities such as good disease resistance and the vigour to produce prolific crops.

Successful pollination depends on insects, especially bees, to carry the pollen from one flower to another. Loss of habitat, pesticides and threats such as the varroa mite, which causes deformity and death among bee colonies, have all led to a drastic decline in the insect population. A mix of trees and flowers that can attract and feed insects, from tiny hoverflies to fat bumblebees, will not only benefit your own apple harvest but make a small yet vital contribution to the health of the natural world.

Rootstocks

As is to be expected, some apple varieties make naturally larger trees than others. Historically, as growers began to experiment with cross-breeding they noticed that if a bud or small stem (the scion) from an over-vigorous variety was grafted on to the rooted trunk (the rootstock) of a smaller-growing variety it kept its flower and fruit characteristics but its growth was limited by the genes of the variety providing the roots. Nowadays, almost all young apple trees sold commercially are grafted on to a rootstock that influences their natural vigour:

ROOTSTOCK	MATURE HEIGHT
M25	5–6 m (16–20 ft) or more
MM111	4–5 m (13–16 ft)
MM106 (or MM116, a similar more recent introduction)	3–4 m (10–13 ft)
M26	2.5–3 m (8–10 ft)
M9	1.8–2.5 m (6–8 ft)
M27	1.2–1.8 m (4–6 ft)

These heights are only a guide, because other factors will affect how large a tree will grow, including the natural vigour of the scion and the fertility of the soil. For example, the rather weak, slow-growing D'Arcy Spice (*see page 60*) is unlikely to reach 3 m (10 ft) on even the semi-vigorous MM111 rootstock, while a Bramley's Seedling on the same rootstock and given the same conditions would probably attain twice that height.

Here are some points to bear in mind when considering which rootstock to choose:

➤ Vigorous rootstocks will sustain a tree better, especially on poor soil.
➤ A tree on an extremely dwarfing rootstock such as M27 will take up less room but require assiduous feeding, watering and staking throughout its life; it will also limit a tree's lifespan to perhaps twenty years or so. Counter-intuitively, M9 or M26 are usually advised for pot-grown plants, rather than M27.
➤ The more dwarfing a rootstock, the earlier the tree will start to fruit. Typically, dwarfing rootstocks will start to produce two to three years after planting, but M25 will take up to six years.
➤ Rootstocks can influence flowering times. A variety on MM106, for example, will flower slightly ahead of the same variety on the very dwarfing M9 or M27.

➤ The rootstock is not the only influence on size: remember to take into account the effect of soil conditions, pruning and other variables. Even the simple measure of growing grass right up to the base of the trunk will have a restricting influence.

One of the most popular all-rounders is the semi-dwarfing MM106, but it may be far from suitable for your conditions. In a very windy location, for example, its roots may not provide sufficient anchorage. MM106 also extends the period of active growth at the beginning and end of the season, which may be a disadvantage in colder areas or frost-prone locations. It has also proved unable to thrive in wetter than average soils and suffers in times of prolonged rain. The rot, literally, sets in. The similar MM116 is not available everywhere, but may prove in time to be a better choice for damp soils. A number of expert growers are now placing greater faith in either M111 or M26, but opinions and experiences differ, so it is wise to take advice from a grower who knows your local conditions.

Occasionally, growers will offer 'interstem' trees, where a third element is brought to the party, grafted between the rootstock and the scion. Additionally, and in complete contrast, there is a school of thought that advocates the benefits of growing trees on their own rootstocks.

Lots to consider, then. The rootstock has a lifelong effect on the tree, so it is worth doing a little homework and taking advice, rather than just going along with what is most readily available. Most fruit tree nurseries will graft on to different rootstocks and can advise you on the best choice for the location and conditions you can provide.

Training

The spectacular sight of a large, spreading apple tree – or even better, a whole orchard – engulfed in a cloud of pink-white blossom is a wonder to lift the spirits, but a full-sized tree takes up a lot of room and can be difficult to harvest and maintain. However, apple trees are very amenable to training into shapes that are both decorative and practical. Some forms of training also make growing apples a realistic possibility in even a tiny garden.

Tree-shaped trees   These are described as STANDARD, HALF-STANDARD or BUSH depending on their trunk height. A standard will develop a clear trunk of about 180–200 cm (6 ft), a half-standard around 120–150 cm (4–5 ft) and a bush (sometimes called a dwarf bush) only around 75–100 cm (2½–3 ft) before the branches begin.

A PYRAMID is also a free-standing tree, but trained to grow in a conical shape rather than a loose lollipop. This is an aid to ripening as the lower branches are not overshadowed by the upper branches. A SPINDLEBUSH is shaped using a different technique but the result is similar.

If you want a specimen tree in the lawn, or are planning a small orchard, remember that you will not want branches so low that they are difficult to mow beneath.

Cordons   These are trained as a single stem, so several could be grown in a short run. Often they are trained at an angle (OBLIQUE CORDON) and tied in to wires, either free-standing or against a wall. A DOUBLE CORDON, giving twice as much growth per tree, is shaped rather like a tuning fork, with two parallel stems that break from a very short central trunk.

Espaliers   Espaliers are formed of tiers of horizontal branches – typically between three and five – making a tightly trained ladder-like arrangement. They can be grown against a wall or fence, or several free-standing trees in a row can make an effective divider or alternative to a hedge within a garden.

Step-overs   Step-overs are just espaliers that are stopped after a single rung, to form a squat T shape, often extending quite wide laterally. A row of them can provide an attractive low border to a path or bed.

Fans   As the term suggests, fan trees are trained into a two-dimensional splay. Espaliers and fans allow for a potentially greater crop than cordons or step-overs while giving plenty of light and air around all the fruit. They look particularly effective against a wall, where they can also benefit from the extra warmth and shelter, something gardeners have appreciated since Roman times.

Fancy shapes   Of course there is no need to stop at these basic shapes. Cordons can be adapted to form CANDELABRA or LATTICES. The ribs of a fan do not have to be straight; they can be trained into curves or whorls for a living wall sculpture. Espaliers or cordons can be trained to form an ARCH, either singly or in an avenue to create a COVERED WALK. All these shapes and more fanciful ones were particularly popular in formal French gardens and then copied in Britain in the seventeenth century.

Training your own tree   Fruit nurseries usually supply specimens two or three years old that have already been given their early formative training, but if you would like the challenge of training a tree from the start, ask for a 'maiden' or a 'feathered maiden'. This is a very young tree that is just a single, whippy stem – or, in the case of a feathered maiden, with a few side stems – grafted on to an appropriate rootstock, waiting to be formed into whatever shape you wish. Choose a specimen that has active buds at the approximate points where you wish your stems to develop. There are many books and videos explaining the steps towards whatever final shape you wish to achieve. See also PRUNING (*page 233*).

Spur-bearing or tip-bearing?

The majority of apple trees develop their fruit buds on short stubby stems, called spurs, along their branches. Some, however, are inclined to fruit in clusters at the tips of the branches. This is not a completely either/or habit – varieties *tend towards* tip- or spur-bearing on a spectrum, and some described as tip-bearing also produce many spurs.

A tendency towards tip-bearing becomes important if you are planning to train your tree into a particular shape. A pruning regime that entails removing all the branch tips of a tip-bearer won't result in much fruit! So strongly inclined tip-bearers that don't produce many spurs are less suitable, for example, to grow as cordons or espaliers, unless you are a very experienced grower.

Growing an apple tree in a pot

Apple trees are not natural pot-dwellers, but by choosing carefully and with a little extra cosseting you can have the satisfaction of harvesting apples even on a balcony or in a soil-less backyard.

- Marry a naturally small-growing variety with a dwarfing rootstock (*see page 223*). Talk to a specialist supplier about choices and aftercare.
- Your tree will eventually need as large a container as you can accommodate: it is going to struggle in anything less than about 45 cm (18 in.) wide and deep. However, it may need to start life in a smaller pot: unused compost in too large a pot will go sour if the root system is not developed enough to aerate it, and the result will be a sad, waterlogged, maybe dead, young apple.
- Follow the general planting instructions above, using a good-quality soil-based compost recommended for shrubs (such as John Innes No. 3), with some added perlite or grit to ensure the drainage is good.

Plants in containers are under greater stress than plants in the open ground.

- Check the compost regularly and when it is dry (feel down into the compost, not just the surface) give a thorough watering – a daily splash 'to be on the safe side' is not the way to go; that will either lead to the roots growing upwards towards the moisture or to unintended waterlogging, something all apples hate.
- The roots will not be able to reach out to find nutrients for themselves. Feed with slow-release capsules or a liquid feed (such as one suitable for tomatoes) according to the manufacturer's instructions.
- Repot with fresh compost every other year. If your tree is in danger of becoming pot-bound, but can no longer be moved on to a larger pot, it can be carefully root-pruned every few years. Continue to replace a proportion of its compost each year.
- Be especially alert to the first signs of pests or disease (*see page 238*), to which a pot-grown plant will always be more vulnerable.

Planting & nurturing

Preparing the site

Apple trees can easily outlive the planter, so give yours a good start in life; you will be repaid a hundredfold.

The ideal site would be sheltered and sunny, with deep, fertile neutral soil, neither too free-draining nor prone to waterlogging and not in a frost pocket. That's the Goldilocks, 'everything just right' scenario, but not the one most typical gardens can provide. But it is worth doing what you can to improve the site; as long as you are not hoping for bumper crops from a tree in a sunless corner of a soggy plot or on a rocky, wind-blasted outcrop, then there is hope.

➨ Look at the site critically, and be realistic about its shortcomings. Choose a variety and a rootstock that will be suited to what you can offer.

➨ Consider how the site might be improved. Would a hedge, however informal, provide a helpful windbreak? Will there be plenty of flowers around to attract pollinating insects?

➨ A specimen tree in the middle of a large bed makes a beautiful focal point, but will you be able to access it at harvest time when the surrounding plants are in full growth? A wall-trained tree can easily suffer from lack of water from being in the wall's 'rain shadow'. Would a buried seep hose or similar contraption be a useful aid?

➨ Most soils can be improved, but do this in advance and over a wide area, not just where you will be digging your planting hole(s) – the idea is to encourage the new trees' roots to develop and spread out in search of nutrition, not for them to hang around the planting hole because it's providing everything they need!

→ Dig the area over well, breaking up heavy clay soils to a good depth and adding coarse, well-rotted garden compost or similar fibrous matter to improve drainage. The same additions, and maybe a little bonemeal, will also nourish a shallow or impoverished soil (loose, sandy soils are inclined to be poor as they cannot hold on to nutrients as well as denser loams). Over-acid soils can be limed. This will not last forever, but will be enough until the young trees are established.

→ If you are planning an orchard, you may envisage a picturesque carpet of grasses and wild flowers beneath your trees. For the first two or three years, however, keep a ring of clear earth around each tree, until they are sufficiently well established not to suffer from competitors for nutrients and water.

→ Think ahead and allow room for your tree(s) to grow. So many garden plants – and not just fruit trees – suffer from being uprooted and replanted, over-pruned or simply discarded because nobody spent ten minutes measuring or pacing out the space they would be likely to take up after a few years.

Planting

The best time to plant a bare-rooted young tree is when it is dormant, from late autumn to early spring, but not in frosty weather. There is more leeway with trees that have been grown in containers.

Stand the tree in a bucket of water for at least a couple of hours. While it is having a good long drink, dig the planting hole. Your preparatory digging (*see above*) should mean the soil is not compacted, so make the hole just deep enough to bury the roots to their previous depth – obvious with a container-grown plant, but you should also be able to see a soil 'tidemark' at the base of the trunk on a bare-rooted plant.

An option at this point is the addition of mycorrhizal fungi. These are sold as desiccated grains which, when sprinkled into the planting hole so that they come into direct contact with the roots, will rehydrate in the moist soil, latch on to the tree's roots and very quickly develop a web of fine filaments that extends much more widely than the tree's own root system. The young tree is then able to benefit from the supplementary nutrient-absorbing network the fungi provide. When using mycorrhizal fungi, follow the instructions carefully, and remember that, although the fungi can be a helpful aid, they are no substitute for good soil conditions and careful planting.

Hold the tree upright in the planting hole and at the right depth, checking that the graft point won't be below soil level. The graft point, where the scion (the upper part of the tree) was grafted on to the rootstock, should be easily identifiable near the base of the trunk. A second person is really helpful, if not vital, at this stage, to hold the tree in position until planting is complete.

Backfill the hole with the soil you have dug out. Firm it down well, checking again that the graft point is not buried. Water thoroughly: unless the soil is already wet, use a full watering can or bucketful to give it a good drench.

Staking and protecting

Staking a newly planted tree will help ensure it grows vertically and not at an angle, and will also prevent it from rocking too much in the wind, disturbing the roots before they have developed a good system. In the majority of cases, it should be only a temporary measure.

The stake should be sturdy and driven well into the ground. Angle it at about 45 degrees from the vertical, so that you aren't driving the point through the precious newly planted roots. Use a soft strap to attach the trunk loosely quite low on the stake. Alternatively, strap the trunk to a pair of vertical stakes either side of the tree, outside the root area. Either system will allow the tree to move but not excessively, so it can build up greater strength and resilience (a false analogy, but imagine it as resistance training for its muscles…). Remove the stake(s) once the tree has established its stabilizing roots, after two or three years.

The exception to this is a tree on a very dwarfing rootstock, whose roots will never develop sufficiently to provide a reliable anchor. As it will require lifelong staking, it may be easier and aesthetically more pleasing to construct a permanent support before planting begins.

Driving wind is not the only threat to a tree's safety. Until your tree has grown a tough, mature bark it will be very vulnerable to gnawing and nibbling – in even a semi-rural area, word will get out to the local voles, rabbits and deer before you have had time to put your spade away! Choose a suitable tree guard to protect the trunk, at least in its early years, or permanently if deer are a problem. Town and country foxes both love fruit, so if they visit your garden you may have to devise some form of temporary protection each year if you are not to lose fruit from low-growing branches.

Labelling

Never assume that you will remember the name of every tree, or even one tree, thirty years or so after planting. Plastic labels are a useful temporary measure, but soon become brittle and illegible (permanent markers do fade with time), so find a more permanent form of record that pleases you, perhaps either an annotated plan or hard-wearing, long-lived labels. When you move on, the next owners will thank you too.

Feeding and watering

A healthy tree will crop more prolifically and better weather any disease or pest attack. Proprietary fertilizers consist of nitrogen (N) for general growth, phosphorus (P) for root growth and flower and fruit development, and potassium (K) for overall strength and health, as well as various trace elements. The proportions of each will be indicated on the label as N:P:K. Apples benefit from a potassium/phosphorus-rich fertilizer formulated for flowers and vegetables. They also respond well to bonemeal, and to chicken droppings – if real chickens scratching around is not a realistic option, poultry manure also comes handily processed, pelleted and bagged.

The best time to feed is in late winter/early spring just before the new season's growth begins. Follow the manufacturer's instructions and don't be tempted to think that more is better – a lush, overfed tree (especially one given access to too much nitrogen) will be less resilient, produce too much sappy growth and be a magnet for aphids, among other problems.

Early spring, while the soil is still moist, is also a good time to mulch. A layer of well-rotted manure, home-made compost or leaf mould, or composted bark around the tree will delay evaporation from the earth. Nutrients in the mulch will also slowly leach into the soil, enriching it; and in time, thanks to weather and worms, the fabric of the mulch itself will be drawn into the soil too, further improving its texture and composition. Spread a broad swathe under the tree canopy, but don't bring it close to the base of the tree itself; mulch may look and feel innocuous but it can scorch or rot bark. A ring of earth left bare around the trunk may also help deter voles – they relish the roots and bark of young trees and can do a great deal of damage, and mulch provides them with cover from predators.

It is important that the soil around a new tree does not dry out, but do treat it to a periodic drenching, not a daily sprinkle, to ensure that the water penetrates to below the root ball, where it is needed. And remember that apples hate to be waterlogged. Once established, after a year or two, they can look after themselves unless they are in containers or an exceptionally poor, dry soil.

Thinning

In good years apple trees often produce far too prolifically to give all the fruitlets a chance to expand and ripen as they should. Nature adjusts to this by shedding a proportion of them in what is called the 'June drop' (which may or may not happen in June), but if pollination has been good you may have to give nature a helping hand.

Wait until the natural June drop has occurred, and then take off any excess fruitlets with a pair of thin scissors or secateurs. Begin with any that are blemished or misshapen and then continue to thin back to the best, to leave just one apple every 5–8 cm (2–3 in.).

Sacrificing so many fruit may seem drastic, but it has several advantages. It will allow the remaining apples better access to sunshine and nutrients, improving the flavour; it could prevent branches snapping under the weight of too many apples; and it will lessen the general strain on the tree. It can also help correct trees that have got into a biennial rhythm: if a tree has a bumper crop one year, it will be inclined to take a rest the following year and then get into a rhythm of fruiting only every other year. Some varieties naturally incline towards this biennial tendency.

Pruning

Pruning makes people nervous. Is it complicated? Will I spoil the tree or lose the fruit by cutting off the wrong stems at the wrong time? Do I need special tools? Don't be put off – pruning is not an arcane ritual; it is just a practical means to an end, and largely comes down to common sense.

There are two things to know about pruning: how to do it, and why. Understanding the 'why' helps make sense of the 'how'.

We prune apples (and most other fruit trees) for two simple reasons: to keep the tree healthy and to encourage a good crop of fruit. In practice this means:

➤ taking out any diseased stems or branches; this includes snapped or damaged stems where disease might enter;
➤ preventing the tree from developing a congested mass of small twigs that will inhibit decent-sized fruit and block sunlight;
➤ training and then maintaining the tree in the shape we wish, to maximize flowering and fruiting.

Pruning is a skill, like riding a bike or swimming, that is easier to do than be told how to do. Below are a few basic guidelines, but seeing pruning done on real trees makes much more sense of the process than a description or diagrams of theoretical trees on the page. If you can, go along to a pruning workshop at a local garden or nursery or evening class – you may be surprised at how many of these there are. The nursery that supplied your tree or trees is another helpful source of advice, where the staff can gear the advice to your particular variety and shape. Alternatively, watch a professional demonstrate on a DVD or online.

A few general rules apply:

➤ Cut back to just above a growth bud, so that you do not leave a stub that will die back and potentially attract disease.

- Make a clean cut, leaving behind no stub or tear, and cut at an angle that will deflect rain away from the bud.
- Cut back to buds facing the direction in which you want the new growth to follow – that is, outward-facing. Inward-facing buds will send up growth towards the centre of the tree and make it more congested in time.
- Keep secateurs and saws sharp, and clean them each time you move on to a new tree and after each session.
- Clear away cuttings: dispose of diseased or rotten wood to prevent spreading infection, but clean wood makes good kindling; when dried, apple wood is aromatic and burns well.

Pruning is generally done in the dormant period, just before the tree starts into growth in the spring, but trained shapes such as cordons and espaliers also require summer pruning.

Winter pruning   Your aim is a few strong branches – three to five is ideal – spaced around the main trunk, supporting a nicely balanced framework of healthy upper branches that are not crowded or overlapping. First of all:

- Inspect the tree for signs of disease or rot (*see page 238*). Cut away any affected branches back to healthy wood.
- Take out any that are growing straight up rather than outwards, as they will just contribute to an overcrowded centre.
- Where two branches cross and are in danger of rubbing against each other, take out the weaker or less well placed one.

If you have bought a two- or three-year-old tree its early pruning will have been towards this end. With a younger, untrained tree you will have to make the decision as to which young stems are best placed to provide the tree's main framework.

Subsequently, study your tree each winter. After you have taken out any diseased or ill-placed stems or branches you will see how new growth, made in the course of the season just ended, extends from older, more weathered-looking growth. Cut some of this new growth back by about a third, aiming to create a pleasing, open shape.

Don't be too heavy-handed with pruning. If in doubt about whether a healthy branch needs pruning, leave it. A tree that has lost a lot of top growth will try to replace it by sending out a mass of new shoots that will sap its energy but not contribute fruiting wood.

You will also notice that your tree develops short, stubby side shoots along the length of its branches. These are the fruit-bearing spurs – don't prune them away!

All the above applies to SPUR-BEARING varieties, which is the majority. A minority of apple varieties are inclined, to a greater or lesser extent, to carry their fruit at the ends of branches, and are referred to as TIP-BEARING (*see page 226*). Shortening the new branches will prune away many of the fruit buds, so tip-bearers should be left to develop naturally for the first five years or so (except for taking out any diseased wood or branches that may rub against each other). Prune as needed after that, taking out the oldest branches to leave younger, more vigorous branches up to four years old, as these will be the best fruit producers.

If you need to restore a mature tree that has been left to run wild the same principles apply, but plan the restoration work over two or three years, to reduce the shock to the tree of reducing so much of its canopy.

Summer pruning   Cordons, espaliers and fans, or variations on these forms, will always be trying to put out new growth beyond the confines of the restricted shape in which they are trained. By high summer a small forest of new shoots may need to be cut back to allow sun and air to reach the swelling fruit and to maintain the trained shape.

Wait until these new shoots have begun to turn woody to about a third of their length – pruned too soon they will enthusiastically regrow. Shorten them to leave a stub of about three leaves, plus the ring of leaves around the base. Leave any shoots that are less than about a stretched handspan long, as these may be developing fruit spurs. On a vigorous variety, or in a year with a long growing season, you may need to repeat this a month or so later.

A tree not trained into a restricted shape which is putting on too much growth in a season can also be curtailed with judicious pruning in late summer. Identify the most vigorous side shoots and when they have stopped putting on new growth and started to turn woody, prune them back to about 15 cm (6 in.). This will encourage them to develop fruit rather than growth buds.

Apples to keep

Many varieties of apple store well; indeed, some improve with keeping. But if stored without care they will shrivel and rot.

- First consider whether you have a suitable location: somewhere dark (or at least dim) that is not damp but not too dry, and that can maintain a temperature above freezing but only a degree or two warmer than a fridge. It should also have good air circulation without being draughty. A garage or shed, as long as it is rodent-free, might be suitable.
- You will need trays or drawers on which to lay the fruit. You can buy purpose-made apple racks, but shallow crates or boxes serve well, as do the polystyrene or cardboard trays in which fruit is displayed in shops. Put the fruit away into storage as soon as possible after they are picked.
- Choose only perfect fruit. A bruise, scrape or a minute borehole, even a missing stalk, will allow rot to enter, and depressingly quickly your entire store could be affected.
- Carefully lay the apples side by side, but not touching, in a single layer. You can choose to wrap them first in newspaper or not – a wrapping will cushion them, allowing slightly closer packing, and will be a small aid to conserving moisture, but will make periodically checking each apple for deterioration a fiddlier job.
- If you are harvesting from a number of trees, keep the same varieties together and label them.
- Inspect the apples at regular intervals, and remove any that are showing signs of rot.

It is not a simple choice of eat, store or discard. There are many other ways of preserving apples not perfect enough to store. Slices, chunks and purée all freeze well, and pressing for juice or cider is fun (juice will also freeze successfully). Apples are an excellent ingredient in many jams and jellies, as they are naturally high in pectin, the setting agent. They are ideal for herb jellies, and makes a lovely fruit butter too. They can also be sliced and dried or made into fruit leathers.

Pests, diseases & disorders

It is trite but true that prevention is better than cure. Below are brief details of the more common problems of apples, but bear in mind:

- A healthy, well-grown specimen will combat an infestation or attack better than a struggling one.
- Some varieties of apple are naturally more disease-resistant than others (this is where triploids can come into their own), and certain diseases and disorders are more prevalent in some areas, so choosing an appropriate variety goes a long way towards growing apples successfully.
- Practise good housekeeping: don't let fallen leaves and rotting windfalls lie all winter, providing a perfect breeding site for insects and moulds; don't add infected leaves or cuttings to the compost heap; disinfect pruning tools to prevent potentially carrying disease from one tree to another.

Bitter pit, a disorder rather than a disease, is caused by lack of calcium. It shows first as a pockmarked skin, and in time the entire flesh is flecked through with brown spots and tastes bitter. This is not a problem brought on by a lack of calcium in the soil, but with the tree being unable to make use of it; it is worse in dry conditions or if the tree is deprived of water at critical times. Putting on a lot of fast growth in early years or a heavy crop on an older tree can also lead to a deficiency.

Ensure your tree is getting sufficient water at the roots (a large tree canopy can act like an umbrella, preventing rain from reaching the soil) and use a general, well-balanced fertilizer to avoid overdosing on nitrogen or potassium. If these measures fail to improve the fruit in subsequent years, a calcium nitrate spray can help. If you favour a variety that is prone to bitter pit, it should help to choose a non-dwarfing rootstock, keep fertilizer on the low side and prune only lightly.

Brown rot is the common rot that attacks apples in store, but it can also affect fruit still on the tree. The skin and then the flesh turn brown and soft, and small pale pustules erupt on the skin. Remove any apples as soon as you see they are affected, to prevent the rot from spreading.

Canker is a fungal disease that enters through a wound in the bark – damage from animals, a bad pruning cut or even a broken bud tip can provide a way in for the spores. It eats away at the wood below the bark, causing areas of bark to wither, disfigure and die back. Eventually it will kill the tree, so it is important to prevent it gaining a hold. It prospers in damp conditions, so ensure the soil is well-drained and keep the tree canopy airy and open; cut out any cankerous branches, ideally when the tree and the spores are dormant.

Codling moth   Apple 'maggots' are the larval stage of the tiny codling moth. Once the grub has got into the fruit it is too late, so preventing it reaching that stage is key. Keeping the ground clear of fallen leaves and fruit will deprive the tiny pupae of their winter quarters, reducing their number. Then, in late spring, hang a pheromone trap in the tree to catch male moths. This will not eradicate them, but will indicate whether you have a problem or not. It will also alert you (the trap will come with guidance on this) to the optimum moment to apply a chemical spray, if you wish. A maggot, or the tunnel it has eaten through an apple's flesh, is not very inviting, but it does not affect the rest of the flesh, which remains perfectly good.

Powdery mildew is a fungus infection most serious in dry regions. It shows first as a pale powdery coating on young leaves; unchecked it will spread to the blossom, stunting growth and distorting fruit. The best way of stopping the fungus's life cycle is to pinch out affected new shoots as soon as the mildew is spotted and, during winter pruning, cut out any branch tips that show signs of infection. This will deprive the fungus of its overwintering home.

Scab is a fungus that develops as yellow then dark brown blotches on the leaves. Similar patches on the fruit skin develop into cracks and lesions. This does not affect the flesh beneath, so the fruit can be peeled and eaten, but the apples become highly susceptible to moulds and rots, and the disease weakens the tree as a whole. Scab thrives and spreads in damp conditions – it is much more common in regions with high rainfall. Ensure your tree has good drainage and that the canopy of branches is kept airy and open, so that excess water can evaporate quickly. Deprive the fungus of a winter home among fallen leaves and fruit.

Aphids, a collective term for all those little sapsuckers such as greenfly and whitefly, can be bothersome in some years. They will not do much damage to mature and vigorous trees, but can debilitate young or weak saplings. Either gently rub them off by hand or, if there is a real infestation, wash them off with a jet of soapy water. WOOLLY APHIDS are also sapsuckers, but they go for woody stems rather than young shoots. The white 'wool' which makes colonies so easy to recognize is not the insect itself but a protective covering they secrete. It may withstand the soapy water treatment, so picking off and squashing the small dark bugs is the best answer.

Winter moths   The small green caterpillars feed avidly on leaves in the spring. They then overwinter as pupae in leaf litter and emerge to crawl up the tree's trunk to lay the eggs of the next generation. Grease bands are the answer to breaking this cycle: unlike codling moths, the females are wingless, hence having to crawl. Wrap a band around the trunk from late October until the spring, and remember to apply a band to any stake as well, or the moths will simply use that as a bridge to reach a suitable egg site.

Root decay, which can threaten a tree's life, may occur because of water-logging or an attack of honey fungus or other fungal disease.

Where to see, taste & buy heritage apples

Heritage orchards can be found all around the country: in the grounds of grand country houses, greening corners between urban streets or former wasteland as community orchards, attached to specialist nurseries, rescued from oblivion by dedicated volunteers, and perhaps even in some of your neighbours' gardens. It is impossible to give a full gazetteer, but here are some suggestions for directions in which to start looking... and tasting.

Many historic properties have their own orchards, some with specific links to old varieties: Parham (Sussex); Audley End (Essex), which holds an annual Victorian Apple Harvest; Sulgrave Manor (Oxon), home to the venerable King Lod tree (*see page 124*); Parcevall Hall Gardens, unexpectedly in the heart of the Yorkshire Dales National Park; and Brantwood (Cumbria), the home of John Ruskin, to name just a few.

The National Trust is custodian of many houses with interesting orchards, from Yorkshire's Nunnington Hall to Ardress House in Co. Armagh, and Acorn Bank in Cumbria to Rudyard Kipling's Sussex home, Bateman's. At Woolsthorpe Manor (Lincolnshire) you can see the original tree (a Flower of Kent) under which, legend tells, Sir Isaac Newton conceived the principle of gravity. In London, the seventeenth-century Fenton House presses and sells juice from apples picked in its own small walled orchard. Many properties hold special Apple Day events: check the Trust's website (www.nationaltrust.org.uk) as autumn approaches.

The Royal Horticultural Society (www.rhs.org.uk) offers practical advice and workshops on all aspects of growing, including apples, and hosts annual shows around the country. It has gardens in Surrey, Devon, Essex, North

Yorkshire and, from 2020, Salford, Greater Manchester, all of which grow regional apples, including heritage varieties.

Check out other horticultural establishments too. The National Fruit Collection at Brogdale, near Maidstone (Kent) is one of the world's most comprehensive fruit collections. The NFC (www.nationalfruitcollection.org.uk) is both a scientific centre and a public resource, where you can see and buy fruit trees. University botanic gardens are often home to interesting old trees (Cambridge's is just one that has its own Apple Day). In the walled kitchen garden of West Dean College (West Sussex) you can see many historic varieties of fruit trees and bushes trained into a range of complex formal shapes (www.westdean.org.uk/gardens).

Heritage apples can be found in some unexpected places. Ampleforth Abbey School (Yorks) has 2,500 trees and its own cider mill. Jodrell Bank (Cheshire) focuses is on trees as well as telescopes, with local heritage varieties in the orchard and the national collection of crab apples. Many of the apple trees in London's Olympic Park Orchard are heritage varieties, and one tree was planted for each British gold medallist at the 2012 Paralympic Games.

Local events are many and varied, whether it's Irish Seed Savers' Taste of the Orchard, cider pressing in Devon or nationwide celebrations on or around Apple Day.

Organizations promoting or advising on heritage apples

Just a small selection; explore your own area and online for many more. People's Trust for Endangered Species (ptes.org/campaigns/traditional-orchard-project). The PTES has a far broader remit than simply apples. Its Orchard Project includes much useful information and links to community orchards, fruit events and other subjects of interest throughout the UK. A good first port of call to find out what's in your area.

Common Ground (www.commonground.org.uk), which seeks to encourage us all to engage with our local environment, was responsible in 1990 for initiating the annual Apple Day (on or around 21 October). Their Apple Map, which appeared in 1993, was part of the movement to highlight local produce. The associated England in Particular (www.englandinparticular.

242

info) is a mine of information, with many links to community orchards and local pomological enterprises.

The Marcher counties (traditionally the lands along the English–Welsh border), including Herefordshire and Worcestershire, were a prime fruit-growing region. The Marcher Apple Network (www.marcherapple.net) is dedicated to preserving and rehabilitating orchards, and especially to tracking down and definitively identifying 'lost' varieties and bringing them back into cultivation. (The MAN also publishes a CD of seventy-seven coloured plates from *The Herefordshire Pomona*.)

A brief special mention must be made here, too, of one particular organization in the Marches: the Woolhope Club (www.woolhopeclub.org.uk). This is the club that originated and published *The Herefordshire Pomona*. Founded in 1851 as the Woolhope Naturalists Field Club to study local flora and fauna, it continues to thrive and contribute to the study of the history, geology and archaeology, as well as the natural history, of Herefordshire and beyond.

A small selection of growers specializing in heritage apples

- Ashridge Nurseries, Castle Cary, Somerset: www.ashridgetrees.co.uk
- The Apple Factor, Dursley, Gloucestershire: apple.sarahjuniper.co.uk
- Bernwode Fruit Trees, Ludgershall, Bucks: www.bernwodeplants.co.uk
- Blackmoor, Liss, Hants: www.blackmoor.co.uk
- Chris Bowers & Sons, Wimbotsham, Norfolk: www.chrisbowers.co.uk
- Frank P. Matthews, Tenbury Wells, Worcestershire: www.frankpmatthews.com
- Harley Nursery, Shrewsbury, Shropshire: www.harleynursery.co.uk
- Heritage Fruit Tree Co., Twyford, Oxon: www.heritageappletrees.com
- Heritage Fruit Tree Nursery, Co. Leitrim, Ireland: heritagefruittreenursery.com
- Herons Folly Garden, Mayfield, East Sussex: www.heronsfollygarden.co.uk
- Keepers Nursery, West Farleigh, Kent: www.keepers-nursery.co.uk
- Ken Muir, Weeley Heath, near Clacton-on-Sea, Essex: kenmuir.co.uk
- Orange Pippin Fruit Trees: www.orangepippintrees.co.uk
- Plants with Purpose & Appletreeman, Bankfoot, Perthshire: plantsandapples.com
- Real English Fruit, Braiseworth, Suffolk: realenglishfruit.co.uk
- R.V. Roger, Pickering, North Yorkshire: www.rvroger.co.uk.
- Scottish Fruit Trees, Glasgow: www.scottishfruittrees.com
- Walcot Organic Nursery, Pershore, Worcestershire: walcotnursery.co.uk

References &
further reading

A facsimile of *The Herefordshire Pomona* is available from the Folio Society, www.foliosociety.com.

The following provided FACTS, FIGURES & INSIGHTS into pomological pursuits past and present:

Bunyard, Edward, *The Anatomy of Dessert* (1929), Modern Library, New York, 2006

DEFRA research project report (GC0140), *Fingerprinting the National Apple & Pear Collections*, DEFRA, London, 2010

Haggard, H. Rider, *Rural England: Being an Account of Agricultural and Social Researches Carried Out in the Years 1901 & 1902*, vol. II, Longmans, Green, London, 1906

Lindley, John, *Pomologia Britannica*, 1841; https://books.google.co.uk

Lysons, Daniel, 'Market Gardens in London', in *The Environs of London*, Volume 4: *Counties of Herts, Essex and Kent*, T. Cadell and W. Davies, London, 1796, pp. 573–6; *British History Online*, www.british-history.ac.uk/london-environs/vol4/pp573-576 (accessed 11 July 2018)

National Apple Congress, *British Apples*, 1883: https://babel.hathitrust.org/cgi/pt?id=coo.31924074140686

National Fruit Collection database: www.nationalfruitcollection.org.uk/search.php

Royal Horticultural Society (RHS): www.rhs.org.uk

RHS Lindley Library: 'Studies in the history of British fruit, in honour of the 150th anniversary of Robert Hogg's Fruit Manual', 2010; www.rhs.org.uk/about-the-rhs/pdfs/publications/lindley-library-occasional-papers/volume-4-oct-2010.pdf

Watson, William, 'An Orchard Survey of the City of Worcester', Worcester Biological Records Centre, 1999

A medley of helpful WEBSITES, mostly giving a more individual viewpoint:

adamapples.blogspot.com – detailed and personal taste notes from an American
   enthusiast
www.applejournal.com/fruitwise – Hampshire-based Stephen Hayes, who has also
   made a number of helpful short YouTube videos: www.youtube.com/channel/
   uc4nsukbotjbtpvnnxmmfpja
www.fruitforum.net – the wide-ranging and always informative site of the 'Queen
   of apples', Joan Morgan
www.gardenappleid.co.uk – Isle of Wight-based, with ID aids that include detailed
   paintings and annotated sketches
www.gardenfocused.co.uk – useful, detailed information and practical advice
www.orangepippin.com – very wide coverage, with input from back-garden
   growers around the world
www.theorchardproject.org.uk – wide-ranging help for community orchards
www.orchardrevival.org.uk – championing traditional orchards in Scotland
www.suttonelms.org.uk/apple1.html – an eclectic site from a hands-on
   Leicestershire pomophile with good information on some less-grown varieties

A short selection from a myriad BOOKS to recommend for further reading,
some practical, others poetic:

Brown, Pete, *The Apple Orchard: The Story of Our Most English Fruit*, Penguin Books,
   London, 2016
Chevalier, Tracy, *At the Edge of the Orchard*, Borough Press, London, 2016
Clark, Michael, *Apples: A Field Guide*, Whittet Books, Stansted, 2015
Jacobsen, Rowan, *Apples of Uncommon Character*, Bloomsbury, New York, 2014
Juniper, Barrie, and David J. Mabberley, *The Story of the Apple*, Timber Press,
   Portland OR, 2006
King, Angela, and Sue Clifford: *Community Orchards Handbook*, Green Books/
   Common Ground, Dartington, 2011
McMorland Hunter, Jane, and Chris Kelly: *For the Love of an Orchard: Everybody's
   Guide to Growing and Cooking Orchard Fruit*, Pavilion Books, London, 2010
Morgan, Joan, and Alison Richards, *The New Book of Apples: The Definitive Guide to
   Apples, Including over 2,000 Varieties*, rev. edn, Ebury Press, London, 2002
Paston Williams, Sara, *Apples*, National Trust/Pavilion Books, London, 2009
Sanders, Rosie, *The Apple Book*, Frances Lincoln, London, 2010
Short, Brian et al., *Apples & Orchards in Sussex*, Action in Rural Sussex, Lewes, 2012
Stocks, Christopher, *Forgotten Fruits: The Stories behind Britain's Traditional Fruit and
   Vegetables*, Random House, London, 2008

Acknowledgements

I am grateful to many people for generously giving me their time, and for sharing their knowledge and enthusiasm for all things apple. First, I must thank Hamid Habibi and his wife Sima, of Keepers Nursery, who were so courteously welcoming on a hot June day, and have been so helpful and enlightening since. Jim Arbury, of the RHS Gardens, Wisley, is another who has kindly come to my aid more than once with his wide knowledge and expertise. My thanks, too, to Derek Tolman of Bernwode Fruit Trees, for his encouragement and advice.

Other head gardeners and nursery owners who have been helpful include: Toby Beasley, at Osborne House on the Isle of Wight; Jim Buckland, formerly at West Dean, and his successor Tom Brown, formerly at Parham; Des Cotton at Glamis Castle; Kevin O'Neil of Walcot Organic Nursery, Pershore; Graeme Proctor of Crown Nursery, Suffolk; Patrick Treherne of Herons Folly, East Sussex.

Advice and answers have come from a variety of other sources too: Nigel Deacon (Sutton Elms – quirky treasure trove of a website, Nigel!); Lorinda Jewsbury, Horticultural Curator at the National Fruit Collection, Brogdale; David Morrell for confirming how his creation, Rambo, got his name; Julia Peel in Tolleshunt d'Arcy; Ainsleigh Rice, Wade Muggleton and Mike Porter at the Marcher Apple Network (so impressed with your detailed knowledge); Ann Smith at the Gloucestershire Orchard Trust. Last but certainly not least, I am grateful to Samuel Fanous for introducing me to *The Herefordshire Pomona* and setting the ball rolling.

Index

249